# Women Code Breakers

## The Best Kept Secret of WWII

### Elise Baker

Intrepidas Publishing

© Copyright 2022 - **All rights reserved.**

The content contained within this book may not be reproduced, duplicated or transmitted without direct written permission from the author or the publisher.

Under no circumstances will any blame or legal responsibility be held against the publisher, or author, for any damages, reparation, or monetary loss due to the information contained within this book, either directly or indirectly.

Legal Notice:

This book is copyright protected. It is only for personal use. You cannot amend, distribute, sell, use, quote or paraphrase any part, or the content within this book, without the consent of the author or publisher.

Disclaimer Notice:

Please note the information contained within this document is for educational and entertainment purposes only. All effort has been executed to present accurate, up to date, reliable, complete information. No warranties of any kind are declared or implied. Readers acknowledge that the author is not engaged in the rendering of legal, financial, medical or professional advice. The content within this book has been derived from various sources. Please consult a licensed professional before attempting any techniques outlined in this book.

By reading this document, the reader agrees that under no circumstances is the author responsible for any losses, direct or indirect, that are incurred as a result of the use of the information contained within this document, including, but not limited to, errors, omissions, or inaccuracies.

# Contents

1. Introduction ... 1
   Cryptology in a Tiny Nutshell
2. Elizebeth Friedman: Not Just a Wife ... 9
   Her Early Life
   Her Career
   Her Legacy
3. Genevieve Feinstein: A Mind For Math ... 24
   Her Early Life
   Her Career
   Her Legacy
4. Joan Clarke: Hidden Gem ... 38
   Her Early Life
   Her Career
   Her Legacy
5. Mavis Batey: Codebreaking Landscaper ... 52
   Her Early Life
   Her Career
   Her Legacy
6. Florence Violet McKenzie: None Like Mrs. Mac ... 63

Her Early Life
  Her Career
  Her Legacy

7. Coral Hinds: Not Alone 82
  Their Early Lives
  Their Careers
  Their Legacies

8. Conclusion 105

About the author 112

Also By 114

Image References 117
  Acknowledgments

References & Bibliography 119

Endnotes 127

# Chapter One

## Introduction

*It is perfectly natural for the future woman to feel indignant at the limitations posed upon her by her sex. The real question is not why she should reject them: the problem is rather to understand why she accepts them.*

—Simone de Beauvoir

This is not a book about how women saved the world, nor is it a book about the excessive tragedies of world wars. It is not even a book about the core science of cryptology. No, it is none of that. What this book does unravel is, in fact, the discovery of a woman's strength through her inevitable involvement in the strategy of war.

This is a story about how women were able to infiltrate the professional world of men by no other means than their own wit, grit, and perseverance.

The stage was set for mayhem and loss, but it was a stage where women were needed for something other than their breeding ability and their homemaking skills.

In this brief and brutal time where inclusivity, duty, and respect took precedence over social norms, a door opened for women to achieve and evolve. This influence was certainly significant in World War One (WWI), yet groundbreaking in World War Two (WWII).

Whether it was manual labor, or selection for specific skills, women were involved everywhere; relieved temporarily from the expectancy of traditional roles to begin quickly and efficiently building, nursing, fixing, training, driving, testing, and filing. Women also did far more clandestine work in the name of duty.

Unfortunately, as the war ended, so did many of these women's wartime purposes. Countless mothers, sisters, and daughters quietly shifted back into their normal lives under their pre-war preconceptions, while very few stayed within their government systems.

Depending on where they were stationed during the war, women were either able to recall their experiences loudly and proudly during the six years of madness (five years for the US), or they were fated to keep it a secret for the rest of their lives and remain hidden from the core truths of history. A past that was quarantined, through patriotic oaths of silence and the undeniable sexism of the time and since.

Revealing that hidden part of history to the world is crucial and long overdue.

As early as WWI (1914-1918), women showed what they were capable of in fields of crypto espionage, pioneering and engineering many of the crypto communication and cybersecurity systems we know today.

There were more than 20,000 women in total recruited to work on top-secret deciphering teams in the United States (U.S.), Great Britain (GB), and Australia during WWII (1939-1945). If they were not breaking and making ciphers, then they were building and innovating the technology that allowed information to move so quickly.

*Women Code Breakers* will bring to your attention the lives of these intelligent, resourceful, and undiscovered women who broke the toughest codes, and far more rigid barriers of self-worth and dignity.

And it is here that we can introduce the women who made it happen. In the next six chapters, we will uncover the lives of:

Elizebeth Friedman: Not Just a Wife

Genevieve Grotjan: A Mind for Math

Joan Clarke: Hidden Gem

Mavis Batey: Codebreaking Landscaper

Violet McKenzie: None Like Mrs. Mac

Coral Hinds: Not Alone

We will be expanding on their early lives, their career successes and failures, and most importantly, their legacy. To wrap up, we will bring to light three more hidden histories of women involved in top secret code breaking work in Australia.

And this is only the beginning. Keep an eye out for other books in the series of *Brave Women Who Changed the Course of WWII*, which shed light on the countless other roles that women played during the Second World War, and what that means for modern women today.

Before we can even begin talking about how they made their careers bloom in this cryptic field, we must first understand the history and science (in the most basic terms) of cryptology and what our silent women heroes were actually doing in those secret rooms.

# Cryptology in a Tiny Nutshell

*Figure 1: The Colossus Computer on display at the National Museum of Computing*

It is easier to break down the basics of cryptology if viewed initially by our current understanding of secrecy, privacy, and cybersecurity. Today, everything is in the "ether": encrypted in bits and bytes, zooming amazingly fast from one corner of the world to another, passing through security system after security system, all ensuring that information remains private.

We are cripplingly dependent on this service that we barely ever see. It works behind the scenes, away from view, within another sector of life. It allows us to get on with our fast, busy 21$^{st}$-century lives, but it does not want to be seen, analyzed, or even queried.

These complex digital systems that protect our information today came from a far more analog and simpler time of classic cryptography: when women and men made and broke codes with a pencil, a paper pad, and a pragmatic attitude. But what about it?

The field of cryptology and the technology surrounding it is a faction of history that seems *to want to be forgotten.* It comes as no surprise that cryptology is a science quite happy to be left dark and dusty in some old library somewhere, locked under top-secret seals of government.

However, the utter injustice comes in when we see countless figures and faces involved at the time being stored away with past historical pieces as well. To also be forgotten in boxes, never to be recognized for their true service to their respective countries.

These records are slowly being released from the National Archives, and every year something interesting and new pops out of the woodwork. Historians have thus quickly come to surmise that the majority of these faces were women.

We know that the evolution of cryptographic (a study and creation of hidden communication) and cryptanalytic (the attempt to break and find weakness in such communication) study spans thousands of years. Humans have been keeping secrets for as long as signals, sounds, and drawings have been around, and most likely will be a part of our civilization for the rest of time.

Historians are keenly aware of the theory that language itself is a form of cryptology. Encrypting a message— that only a small handful of other people know how to interpret— is vital to success in groups, so it was vital to the success of nations at war.

Its tactical use in history is popularized by the Roman emperor Julius Caesar, who would write encrypted messages to his generals, preventing spies from learning of their plans. This came to be known as the Caesar Cipher or Caesar Shift.

It works like this. You take a simple word like, let's say, CAESAR! You write out the word (called plaintext), and then begin shuffling each letter in a particular pattern so that if it is intercepted by a stranger, it looks like total gibberish. Something like ZBXPXO. This is called encryption or creating a ciphertext.

Now the only person who should be able to read this cryptograph is the intended receiver as they know both the cipher rules and the key.

The <u>cipher</u> is the set of rules that are used to encode the plaintext. For instance, to decode the message, the rule is to shift the placement of letters in the alphabet by a certain amount. That certain amount would be the <u>key</u>.

In a Caesar Shift, the key is always three. When encoding, you move each letter directly *three spaces down* (left rotation) in the 23-letter English alphabet, such as E becoming B, and R becoming O. Thus, when decoding, you have to move those letters *three spaces up* (right rotation) in the English alphabet.

Here is a cryptograph for you to decipher if your wish to test your skills:

EBV OBXABO. VLR OLZH!

This is one of the most common monoalphabetic ciphers, a class of cipher that requires simple one-to-one substitution. The encryption is a subtraction and the decryption is an addition, where each letter is a number. This means A equals 0, B equals 1, C equals 2, and so forth. By doing simple modular arithmetic, you can decipher the code much faster, giving us over 400 septillion different ways to encrypt this plaintext.

This method was applied and modified into more complex and differentiative ciphers. As technology developed between WWI and WWII, so did cryptology and the spy network. Harder polyalphabetic ciphers were composed, like Playfair cryptography, or the Vigenére cipher, where various different substitutions and multiple rules were needed to decipher the code. Rules upon rules within different spaces and letters, shifting letter pairs instead of singular letters.

If a cryptanalyst did not know the key nor the rules of the cipher, then they would attempt to crack the code. This was either done by a trial-and-error method called Brute-Force, which requires lots of time, data, and patience to go through all the various combinations before you find the correct one, or through reverse deciphering by working backward from the encrypted message.

Later a more refined method of deciphering was developed, called Frequency Analysis. To explain frequency analysis, think about the most common letters in the English alphabet. These would be the letter E, the letter T, and the letter A. These will have far greater frequency than, say, the letter Z, in any given sentence.

Cryptanalysts would 'connect the dots' of frequency models within the encoded message. The longer the message, the easier it was to decode because you could pick up on the frequency of letters.

These commonalities were called 'cribs' showing where the key created recognizable patterns. This was used by the great minds behind the famous Enigma and Purple machine, which improved time constraints with minimum resources.

Is it possible to create a cipher that is technically unbreakable? The answer is yes, and they did. It is called a one-time pad encryption. It was and still is the only unbreakable cipher. This is because the key used for each cipher is always as long as the cipher itself, meaning it is almost impossible to retrieve patterns from the cipher. The sender and the receiver have the exact same pad, with a set of numbers as the key. As each message is encoded or decoded it is destroyed and the same key is never used twice. This very method is a template for the great enciphering machines of WWII.

As the years passed, with wars beginning and ending, the evolution of cryptology was affected by the development of new and ingenious ways to make and break messages. From analog to mechanical, and finally, digital, this science has been fundamentally nurtured by women, as only during and after WWII did the field really begin to make strides.

This is precisely where we can start getting a feel for what is to come. It was a small science before women came along and gave it life. Not something anyone could do, but many women did!

As you venture through the stories in this book you will come to see where our early 20$^{th}$-century women were being stifled; smothered by the dominating opinions of the period, as well as their grace and flexibility in managing injustice. You will see them demonstrate their strength in endeavoring for a greater cause – to bring the Second World War to an end. Despite the horror, violence and tragedy of it all, what a dramatic and exciting time to be alive for our female code-breakers!

Let us start to understand the role early 20$^{th}$-century women truly had in the fields of telecommunication and crypto analytics of WWII.

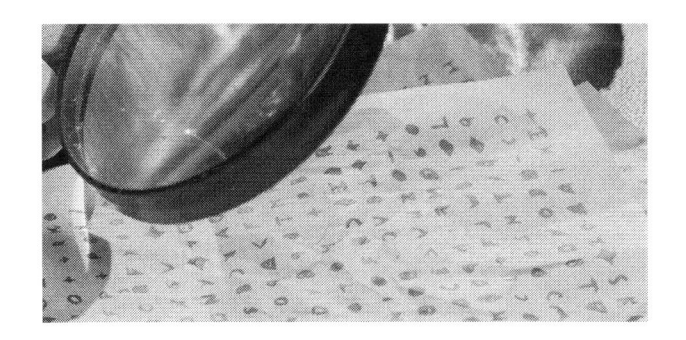

# Chapter Two

## Elizebeth Friedman: Not Just a Wife

*Figure 2: Elizebeth Smith Friedman*

Elizabeth Friedman was left out of history books for many years. She was a brave woman who lived and died with her oath of secrecy intact, carrying the torch as the first American female cryptanalyst.

Historians found out about this woman through her code-breaker husband, William Friedman, and only after looking backward through the life of this man did they find the jewel of his wife. They discovered her true role, not just as a petite wife and mother, but also as a tenacious codebreaker. As the archives opened, it gave us a huge chunk of history that had been silenced for decades.

The director, Chana Gazit, of the PBS documentary *The Codebreaker*, reveals this woman's incredible work saying, "If we missed someone as big as Elizebeth, who else are we missing?" (Oullette, 2021). Well, exactly. Who else has been hidden from view for the sake of official privacy and, perhaps, masculine pride?

## Her Early Life

Elizebeth Smith Friedman came into the world in the Progressive Era of 1892, into a Quaker (Protestant Christians) family on a dairy farm in rural Indiana State. Friedman was the youngest of nine other siblings to father John Smith and mother Sopha. Her mother chose to spell Elizebeth's name with an 'e' instead of the usual 'a' so that people would not call her 'Eliza', which she apparently detested.

Accounts of her childhood shine a light on her determination in everything she did. Friedman was strongly opinionated, objective, and very energetic, whose open face held vivid and clever eyes.

This was the end of the 19$^{th}$ century, a time named the Second Industrial Revolution because of its development of, not industry, but rather of technology and science. This shows the value that was placed on education, even if exclusively for men.

From the age of 19 to 21, Friedman attended the liberal arts school in Ohio called Wooster College. Many young girls from middle-class families were being sent to all-girls schools that gave the basic foundations of English, arts, mathematics, and literature, as well as natural and social science.

It was not always seen as necessary to send girls to school, but certainly helpful if they were to maybe, let's say, meet a young fellow in the neighboring boys' school. Someone affluent who offered good marriage prospects.

These were the ideals of the time, as the education of girls had different criteria at its core. Rather than the pure pursuit of knowledge, it was more of a pursuit of leverage gained when around the 'right sort of people.'

Friedman's mother's sudden illness required her to transfer to a school closer to home and, in 1915, at the age of 23, she majored in English literature and poetry, though she was also keenly interested in Latin, German, and Greek. Her avid passion for poetry would follow her through every important moment in her life, as you will see further into this chapter.

Straight from student to teacher, later that year, she took on the role of substitute principal at a public school in Indiana. She did not stay long in that post, however, and moved back into her parents' house at 24, ready to start something new, yet not too sure what.

## *Not Just Any Trip To Chicago*

On a whim, and just for the sake of getting out of the house, Friedman traveled to Chicago to visit the Newberry Research Library to see an original piece by the famous playwright, William Shakespeare (whom she studied and loved), called *First Folios*.

While there, Friedman tried her luck and asked if there were any positions available at the library. She approached the front desk, and a librarian no older than herself, who was silently filing away an assortment of papers, looked up to greet her. They began exchanging pleasantries and conversing freely about interests, coming to find out that they were both from Indiana and from Quaker families.

Feeling more at ease in the conversation, Friedman explained her reason for visiting and the librarian smiled wildly, exclaiming, "Well! You don't say! I have a friend who, apart from being exuberantly wealthy, is also madly enthusiastic about the works of Shakespeare!" She then added with a raised eyebrow, "Since you are looking for a research position, I will see if we can connect you with dear George Fabyan. Perhaps your common passion for literature can be financially profitable!" Well, of course, she gave it a go. This was a simply amazing opportunity!

In no time, the librarian was on the phone. That very day, a limousine arrived at the library, and that was how Friedman met the eccentric millionaire whose fortune was largely built around the inheritance from his tycoon father's textile business.

Indeed, Fabyan was quite a character, known for doing arbitrary things that made little sense but caused mirth. As author Jason Fagone mentions in his 2021 book *The Women Who Smashed Codes*, "He [Fabyan] wore riding pants all the time even though no one ever saw him on a horse. He called himself a colonel even though he had never served in the military" (Baraniuk, 207, para. 10).

Fabyan whisked Friedman away to the Riverbanks estate, after being chauffeured from one car to another. During the hour trip, he talked wildly about his ideas for his literature department at his Riverbanks research facility in Geneva, Illinois. He didn't fail to tell her that she *would stay* with him and his wife that very night, so he could show her around and convince her to work for him in the Shakespeare deciphering project.

Riverbanks Laboratories was the strangest of places to come upon, even if you saw it today. It had the look of a badly-made wedding cake; topped with levels upon levels of rooms and windows, all culminating in one final space for a roof veranda. Surrounded by beautiful wild gardens in a very lofty estate, this property was certainly out of the ordinary. It also boasted a private zoo, a well-manicured Japanese garden, a greenhouse, a swimming pool envisioned in the typical Roman style with high pillars, and a lighthouse off the nearby lake.

This facility was all about the obscure sciences of the time. In fields like chemistry, genetics, veterinary study, acoustic technology, as well as cryptology, there was a great need for more answers. The cryptography department worked on specific historical pieces of information, looking for clues to their possible secret meanings.

It was 1916, and obviously convinced, Friedman was freshly employed at the facility. She began to work on an intriguing project along with colleagues Elizabeth Wells Gallup and her younger sister Kate; an attempt to de-code the bilateral cipher in Shakespeare's plays. They were tasked with trying to find a secret message within the text that would point to a perceived truth: that a certain Sir Francis Bacon was the real author of Shakespeare's plays. It may sound faintly ridiculous now, but back then, the people who fervently believed this theory became known as Baconians.

At Riverbanks, Elizebeth met William Friedman, a plant botanist, geneticist, and avid cryptologist who trained at Riverbanks as well. During this time, they fell in love, requesting the same shifts and spending much of their off-time together. They had many things in common, including their love for poetry and Shakespeare.

William popped the question in 1917, the same year America declared war on Germany in WWI. They were married hastily and continued living and working on the property as a couple.

Picture her sitting there, in some dusty library at Riverbanks in the late hours of the night, with books piled up over her desk. See her peering down at a page, riveted by her quest, a single light illuminating a page, thinking to herself, *Heavens! What does it mean, and can this actually be deciphered?* She lifts her head and looks over at William who is seated at the opposite desk, never too far away, with a cup of tea, or an understanding nod, and smiles sweetly at the man who would stay by her side for the rest of his life.

There is something incredibly romantic about falling in love at inauspicious times. It is no wonder that movies and books depict these scenarios so often. The challenging circumstances of war induced relationships based on character and determination, which contrasted sharply with norms based on profitability and safety for the majority of people in everyday life.

Friedman's perseverance revealed something special about her, something to marvel at. William saw it straight away. As her career bloomed, she mastered her skills, bringing her husband along for the ride.

## Her Career

George Fabyan received a request from the U.S. government at the onset of WWI to bring forth codebreakers from their staff and have them work at the facility in military codebreaking. Author of *Secret Messages*, David Alvarez, mentions in his book how, "Riverbanks cipher department was the only place in the country pursuing systematic cryptanalysis" (Alvarez, 2000), way before the Central Intelligence Agency (CIA) or National Security Agency (NSA). This gave those few who worked in the cryptography department a real chance to improve and help their country.

Friedman's unusual ability to recognize patterns in incoherent numbers and letters was a natural skill set that made her perfect for the job, picking up the basic principles of cryptology very quickly. She detected spaces and rhythms of text and number groups in a very detailed way, which was honed during WWI, and gave her the platform to develop later through self-study.

As soon as the dark clouds of war started gathering on the horizon, the British chose to share their cryptology knowledge with America (some would say in a desperate attempt) even though there were tensions between the two countries. Great Britain harbored insecurities about whether it was a smart move to start trusting the Americans to keep secrets and become true Allies. It was a delicate situation.

In the United States, as early as the American Revolution, cryptology was already in play within communications between opposite factions of conflict; with letters written between generals and leaders being encoded, but it had not evolved sufficiently in techniques of deciphering.

This field steadily evolved into the onset of WWI in 1914 with the Zimmerman telegram being intercepted by British intelligence. This was the famously intercepted message between Germany and Mexico suggesting that if America went to war, then the Germans would ally with Mexico and conquer the U.S. from the south.

As technology in communication was refined, thanks to electricity spreading all over the world, telephones, telegraphs, radio, and signal lamps became a norm in day-to-day life, and their use became a pathway to innovation, as well as invasion.

The Americans showed their strength and learned fast. They sprinted ahead and grew, aided by the development in 1919 of The Black Chamber by Herbert Yardley. The Black Chamber was a cryptographic division of the Military Intelligence (MI-8) which broke many communications from other countries by opening, reading, and resealing thousands of telegraphs over many years.

For Friedman, it must have been such a refreshing experience because, as Fagone notes, "Gender roles had not become a barrier because there was hardly anyone in code-breaking at all" (Haynes, 2021, para. 5). This left a huge gap for interpretation and experimentation at the time. The cryptography world was in its infancy and there was ample potential for improvement.

## Moving With the Times

As WWI ended and the world fell into the Great Depression, the Friedmans moved out of Riverbanks Laboratories, ready to start something new. This proved to be a rather tiresome affair, as Fabyan had been intercepting their mail, which contained job referrals and acceptances, clearly not wanting the couple to leave.

In 1921, they moved to Washington D.C. to work at the government's War Department and then the U.S. Treasury Department. During this time, the Volstead Act was in effect, prohibiting the manufacture and selling of alcohol. The Prohibition-era proved to be a good time for the Friedmans and their team to improve their skills.

While working for the U.S. Coast Guard over the next 10 years, their team intercepted and monitored countless smuggling rings, cracking down on an estimated 12,000 different enciphered messages between narcotic smugglers and mobsters, also called 'rum-runners'.

Friedman alone was responsible for the encrypted messages from hot spots like Florida and San Francisco and her decryption resulted in the incarceration of the infamous Ezra Brothers' narcotics ring. Over 600 criminal prosecutions were executed thanks to Elizebeth's work, as she sat in court and testified for 33 of them.

This must have been a very exciting and equally draining time for the couple. What we don't read, we must try to comprehend through imagination.

Elizabeth and her husband William were having a cup of coffee one morning, getting ready for the day. Elizebeth looked up from the newspaper and solemnly asked her husband, "William, do you truly think we are making a real contribution to America's future, through the secretive work we do?" William looked over at her kindly with smiling eyes, and said, "Darling, don't worry yourself so. The importance of what we do is only important because it is done secretly. Catching drug smugglers, pointing out Japanese spies, and resolving diplomatic feuds with our neighbor Canada is no small thing. We work silently to end the wars that rage. Let that be enough for now."

Around this time, Friedman started to feel a sort of frustration towards her peers. Deep down inside, she must have understood that her contributions would be overshadowed eventually. Her male colleagues would honorably take the podium in her stead. Swallowing that sort of pride was indeed very brave, even if it was something that she was naturally expected to do.

These cryptology departments were headed by esteemed and noteworthy men, heavily supported by women. Between Washington D.C., London, Sydney, as well as in Moscow, and Chongqing (China), there was a substantial pooling of resources and information as WWII erupted onto the world's stage.

Throughout WWII, Elizebeth's cryptology team, Unit 387, would be under the command of the U.S. Navy. In her previous work with the government, she and her husband were usually in charge of their cryptology unit, but under the Navy, civilian command was prohibited. Around 4,000 women in Washington worked at the naval codebreaking facility, which is now the Department of Homeland Security, and another 7,000 working in Arlington Hall.

This gave her the responsibility of monitoring secretive communications between Germany and South American countries, specifically Chile, Argentina, and Bolivia, while having no authority on the team.

Before the Pearl Harbor bombings in December 1941, there had long been suspicion that there were again efforts from the Axis powers to weaken the U.S. Allies by 'fishing out' the resource-rich Southern American countries from their grip, turning them fascist, and then invading the U.S. from the south.

Friedman and her team spent 18 months intensely focused on intercepting the locations, identities, and code names of Nazi spies through their communications via the famous German Enigma machine (we will delve into this more in Chapter 3). Alan Turing and his team on one side of the pond craftily found ways to decode this 'undecipherable' machine, while Elizebeth and her team were working each message out by hand with a good old-fashioned pen and paper.

## *Power Play*

The Navy worked together with the Federal Bureau of Investigation (FBI) throughout many of the operations in Allied counterintelligence, however, Friedman always managed to butt heads with her 'new friends'.

Friedman believed she was there to do efficient covert work, whereas the FBI, headed by Director J. Edgar Hoover, was stomping around rather loudly, interfering and monopolizing information. These tables were set for hungry men to gain credit - whether it helped or damaged others did not matter. Power play and ego-pushing often interfered with good surveillance.

One day, the worst happened. The Friedmans arrived at work as usual, quite excited about recently locating the headquarters of the South American spy ring, but to their surprise, the usually bustling cover transmissions surrounding the Nazis were eerily quiet.

Elizabeth and William jumped up, hearts pounding, knowing the inevitable. *They've figured out we have been listening in! That's it. Cover over.* This usually meant starting from scratch, as the Germans would quickly change their cipher keys on the Enigma machine.

*But how? What had the team missed?* The answer would come to her infuriatingly quickly, as she would find out that the FBI had unofficially pulled the information of where this spy ring was located, and without informing anyone, raided the premises hastily. This obviously notified the Germans of infiltration, and they went underground in no time.

This little stunt would push Friedman's efforts back for months, as Hoover failed to comprehend how the repercussions would affect their unit, not to mention her pride.

From then onwards she would "redouble her efforts and get back to work" (her usual motto but with a touch of resentment), and with pen and paper, the team deciphered three new Enigma codes which led to the 1942 capture of Nazi high-ranking SS member Johannes Siegfried Becker (code name 'Sargo') and his entire network in South America. This saved the government hundreds of thousands of dollars.

It was not only internal spy counterintelligence in which Friedman dipped her fingers. She also, as did many, consistently intercepted German U-Boat transmissions in the Atlantic and Pacific. (In German, a submarine is "Unterseeboot" (undersea boat), thus, "U-boat.")

These German U-boats would target Allied supply and troopships so as to interfere with the support and monopoly they had over the large bodies of water. The only way to prevent the Germans from sinking their ships was to play a fast game of *Risk* on the Pacific front.

When the codebreaker knew the location of the U-Boat and its target, they would immediately alert the U.S. and British naval leaders to send messages for the Allied ships to drastically change course. Many of these troopships carried more than 8,000 servicemen, meaning that these cryptology teams saved thousands of lives daily. The faster the codes were broken, the longer people lived.

When the war was over, the South America incident became a publicity move that Hoover used to prop himself up in the public eye. He proclaimed the FBI solely responsible for uncovering the Axis powers in South America, even promoting a publicity reel about the incident titled 'The Battle of The United States.' People believed this for many years.

Although she got absolutely no recognition for it, Friedman broke around 4,000 encoded messages during the war. Her husband received great praise for his efforts in an article published in *Time* magazine in 1956, which called him the grandfather of cryptanalysis (a term coined by William), while she stood in the background mentioned solely as an 'assistant cipher clerk.'

This must surely have bruised her pride, as both Elizebeth and her husband knew that she was the person anyone would go to for help with fixing difficult problems. A silenced mastermind, a silent hero, and in truth, a core member of the team. Either way, she shrugged her shoulders and got on with her life.

The end of WWII would bring about her eventual retirement from government code-breaking. She would focus her time on being the mother to her young-adult children, then 22-year-old Barbara and 19-year-old John.

Her immediate family was clueless about her actual role during the war, which did not fit the image of an average suburban wife. She must have been so used to answering questions about her job with, "I'm an office assistant for the government," or, "Oh, nothing much. Although I do enjoy a good puzzle!"

Having signed and promised an oath of silence till the day she died meant exactly that.

The Friedmans' dual passion for literature, specifically that of Shakespeare, later led them to write a book in 1957 titled *The Shakespearean Ciphers Examined*. Here the couple reverted back to the early days at Riverbanks and uncovered the truth behind the incorrect hunch by George Fabyan and the other Baconians that Francis Bacon had secretly written the plays. The couple even cheekily encoded within the book, in bilateral cipher: "I did not write the plays. F. Bacon." The manuscript has been described as written with exceptional finesse and character.

Over the years together, Friedman noticed signs of deep depression in her husband. He started suffering as early as the 1930s, when Elizabeth often had to make excuses for his absence or temperament. In early 1941, William was admitted to a psychiatric ward in Washington D.C. where his condition was assessed as stress from the nature of his work. He suffered several heart attacks from 1955 and his health would deteriorate from then onwards, leaving Elizebeth to take care of him in their home.

William Friedman died at the end of 1969, and Elizebeth spent the remaining years compiling a bibliography of her husband's cryptographic material and handing it over to the Marshall Research Library in Virginia. She was proud of her husband's work, yet reticent about her own.

11 years later, in 1980, and at the age of 88, Elizebeth Smith Friedman died in her nursing home in New Jersey.

Only later in 2008, when the archives opened, were her children and grandchildren able to learn of her legacy and the contributions she made to her country, and the role model she was to countless others.

## Her Legacy

When WWII naval and military archives were declassified in the late 2000s, there must have been a huge sigh of relief from the grave. *Finally! The code of silence is broken*, with Elizebeth Friedman's voice a part of the whole.

She was a true visionary of strategic intelligence and a woman of courage and love who won the world's appreciation long after her due.

The news clippings and journals of the time often portrayed her as an unlikely national hero. Somewhat of a pity that it should be 'unlikely.' A decent, well-groomed woman, with her head screwed on tight, who kept her wits about her and never stopped moving forward. There is nothing unlikely about that. She broke barriers and stepped up at the right time to become the first American female cryptologist and set the stage for the rest to come.

> *You did what you could with what you had to do it with.*
> –Elizebeth Friedman

And she definitely did! Not just teaching herself, but her husband, her colleagues, and the world what genius can lie hidden behind the façade of a quiet, unassuming woman. She blossomed and made the right people look up, even if that was not her primary concern.

She gave so much more, like all the women to come, than was ever recognized. And for that matter, she did not seem to care, either. She was just happy to have done what was needed and lived the life that she created.

In 1999, Elizebeth Friedman was inducted into the NSA Hall of Honor. In 2002, an NSA building was dedicated to the Friedmans. And in 2020, Elizebeth Friedman was named Legend-Class by the U.S. Coast Guard thanks to her legendary status in its history, and the following year they began the construction of the warship *USCGC Friedman*.

Her legacy grows with her natural prowess at mastering the skill of cryptanalysis, although we see something greater when we take a step back and look at the bigger picture: we see a brilliant mind in a caring person, developed by the pressure of hard times.

# Chapter Three

## Genevieve Feinstein: A Mind for Math

*Figure 3: 1935 Buffalonian yearbook: Genevieve Grotjan, Mathematics, Pi Kappa Phi, courtesy of the University Archives, University at Buffalo, The State University of New York.*

Genevieve Grotjan Feinstein was a spark in the early 20ᵗʰ century. She lit up the sky for one brief moment in history, and then faded away, as many of their kind do.

This woman understood the meaning of achievement at a very young age. And she kept that memento throughout her life, influencing many in her wake.

When it comes to the talent and tenacity present in codebreaking, then we cannot forget this American whose accomplishments spoke so loudly, without her having to say anything.

With her achievements over the course of WWII "go[ing] down as a milestone in cryptologic history" (Whitcher Gentzke, 2022, para. 3), we just have to break down the life and legacy of this sweet and bold mathematician.

## Her Early Life

Born in 1913 as Genevieve Marie Grotjan, called Gene by her friends, she came into this world as an only child to pharmacist father Frederick and dutiful homemaker Lilian. They lived in Buffalo in New York State, with Fredericks' parentage linked directly to Germany.

She was what we today would call an overachiever, and able to excel in almost everything she put her mind to. More than anything, she wanted to teach mathematics. At the time, she desired the simple life that was expected of her with a small career in teaching before marrying and becoming a mother. Her path would involve a lot more than that.

People would consider her shy, but she seemed to know exactly where her strengths lay, and she didn't deviate. Feinstein received medals for academic success throughout her childhood and young adult life, her face and name often plastered in newspapers congratulating her on her achievement.

Under a Regents scholarship, she enrolled at the University of Buffalo in 1930. She joined all the clubs that interested her, being secretary of the math club and a member of the German club, music club, as well as the Pi Kappa Phi sorority. A real go-getter!

## *Calculating Her Options*

Feinstein clearly excelled in mathematics, finding a mentor and role model in UB Mathematics Professor Harriet Montague, and winning, in 1934, the William H. Sherk Memorial prize for submitting an incredible projective geometry paper on "Involutions of Pencils in Rays." At the time, this was described as, "the best paper submitted in any branch of mathematics, pure or applied" (Whitcher Gentzke, 2022, para. 9).

In 1936, at the age of 25, she graduated with a mathematics *summa cum laude* at the University of Buffalo with major credits in Latin, physics, and education. While she finished her master's thesis, she was hired as a tutor and substitute teacher in various schools in the area, until she eventually found a promising position as a graduate assistant in the math department of her old university, where she taught analytic geometry and trigonometry.

Feinstein was heading for some great academic heights, being invited to lecture at the National Council of Teachers of Mathematics and elected as a Sigma XI, which was an honor given in science and engineering. She was getting ahead, but failed to finish her thesis at Buffalo University, which evidently had something to do "with the discouraging reaction to her quest for a college teaching post" (Whitcher Gentzke, 2022, para. 10), which might have come across as overstretching boundaries for a woman in her time.

No matter. She managed to complete her graduate work later in life, despite the prevalent limiting beliefs which had previously held her back.

In 1938, for the sake of simply finding something to do, as schools were not hiring, she took a job at the Railroad Retirement Board doing clerical work and calculating pensions. She enjoyed her work but still believed that she would find something within her mathematical fields of interest. She was keeping an eye out for new opportunities.

While Feinstein was calculating pensions and the world was preempting war, the Navy and U.S. Army were consolidating prominent women's colleges to train new personnel in cryptology, knowing that they needed to fill a sector with fresh minds. Men were at war, so women had to take a stand, filling greater Science, Technology, Engineering, Mathematics (STEM) fields and gearing up to enter the workforce.

## Her Career

In records pulled from the Naval archives, there is a single statement in a 1941 report mentioning the conceptualization of female recruitment. At the very bottom of the list, it reads, "New Source: Women's Colleges" (Talks at Google, 2019). Men had run out of options.

In her 2017 book titled *Code Girls: The Untold Story of The American Women Code Breakers in World War II* American author Liza Mundy mentions, in an interview at the National WWII Museum in New Orleans, that "the [recruiters] were looking for young women who had mathematical ability but also were good at languages because that really helps." (Gregg, 2020).

Liberal art schools like Goucher Hall and the Seven Sister Colleges (Radcliffe, Smith, Vassar, Mt Holyoak, Bryn Mawr, Wellesley, Barnard) were not only where they recruited women proficient in mathematics, astronomy, physics, and languages, but where they held many late-night locked-door training sessions to teach them how to decipher enemy codes.

The Navy, being a little pickier than the Army, preferred to recruit women from colleges and schools, looking for gems in the rough, so to speak. The

Army took a wider approach and sent out large recruitment parties around the States at state schools, offices, and teaching colleges.

That is where we see Feinstein impress some key figures in the cryptology sector by achieving a remarkable score in a basic routine service mathematics test. Tests like these were regularly pulled and evaluated by the government sectors to scan and monitor for above-average scores from individuals at universities, colleges, and offices.

One of those key figures was William Friedman. Yes, the very husband of our previous heroine.

The cryptanalyst spotted Feinstein's talents and asked her if she would be interested in joining his team at the Signals Intelligent Service (SIS) in Arlington Hall just outside of Washington D.C. This was a division of the Army Signal Corps created by Friedman and three other affluent male cryptologists to work on counter security in cryptology and communications. SIS would eventually become enveloped under the Army Security Agency after the war and later transferred to the NSA.

At the time, officers were informed to keep an eye out for educated women, although before education came trustworthiness. A memo released in 1942 from the Navy cryptology department by Captain Laurance Safford reads:

> "In view of the confidential nature of the work done in this section, it is essential that all personnel be especially selected for integrity. Individual qualifications are of secondary concern and used only as the basis for assignments after integrity has been established."
>
> (Wilcox, 1998, p. 3)

So, this must have been the process that Feinstein, like all the other women in this book, had to go through. Along with the aptitude and skill testing that involved understanding, studying, and breaking down patterns, they were thoroughly screened, given background checks, and interrogated on their past, motivations, and values in life. Aptitude testing in itself was essentially born at this time when better ways to study intelligence and logic in humans were being devised.

An interesting revelation about the recruitment process was made by Liza Mundy in her book. In many cases a quick introduction to the interview started with two basic questions:

*Do you enjoy doing puzzles?*

*Are you planning on marrying any time soon?*

If they answered the first with a yes and the second with a no, then they would be moved on to the next stage of training. These women needed to be both calm of mind and sharp of eye, capable of working hard under pressure while also being very resilient. There was no time for being discouraged.

*Oh, my – what an offer!* thinks Feinstein. She looks at William Friedman with level eyes, trying to masque her pure excitement, gingerly saying, "All right, Mr. Friedman. Just so I get this straight, you want to employ me in a secretive position with long hours and intensive work?"

A quick and efficient nod from William Friedman is all she needs.

## *Down The Rabbit Hole*

Well, of course, she happily agreed, knowing that she was going to be getting an opportunity to do something great, possibly honorable, even though she did not yet know what this work would consist of.

Oaths of secrecy were signed and contracts displayed. She was given the objective and the tools to get there and was instructed never to forget that it was a crime to speak about her job. This was the case for many of the other women employed within the department. They arrived in Washington D.C. to find that this was an operation that required absolute secrecy. If they spoke of what transpired, that would be prosecuted under the law as treason, punishable by death.

Many thousands of women joined the Women's Army Corps (WAC) and received special life insurance rates, and reduced fees for transport and entertainment only after much deliberation. Before 1941 the designation of 'auxiliary' was used as Women's Auxiliary Army Corps (WAAC), which gave few benefits and no salary to the women that enlisted. Only in 1943 was the designation dropped, allowing women those privileges as well.

General Marshall makes a broadcast in 1944 aimed at the recruitment and motivation of women, saying:

> "The Women's Army Corps is an integral part of the army of the United States. The members are soldiers in every sense of the word and perform a full military part in the war." The general adds, sternly looking into the camera, "As more and more American soldiers engage in enemy combat, women must replace them at overseas bases and at posts in this country. In view of the urgency of the situation, enlistment in the military should take precedence over any other responsibility, except that of imperative family obligation."
> 
> (The Best Film Archives, 2013)

These were the circumstances that ruled the five years of war for the US. It is crucial to remember that even though these thousands of American women were not mathematically inclined or selected for greater tasks like Feinstein, their involvement was just as monumental as hers.

It is also important to state that, at the time, we still see racial segregation. There were African American women working in a separate accounting department with the task of ensuring that no fraudulent or suspicious accounts or financial transactions were taking place. They had a task, and they were included in the efforts, but still under the racial premise of the time.

Many African American men were drafted as well, not only fighting for the freedom of their country but also for the freedom of their racial equality within that very country. Marginalized and positioned as solely support roles, the war would become a large platform for community and national involvement between races.

So, Feinstein trained and learned quickly, fitting well into her position as a junior cryptanalyst in what was called 'the code section' of SIS. Feinstein worked with hundreds of other women and reported to the junior analysts as they went through hundreds of messages daily. Out of 15,000 people employed at SIS, 7,000 of them were women.

These women were often discussed in later years as being a lot like "cogs in a giant machine" (Baraniuk, 2017, para. 20), who sorted and shifted through large amounts of data. And many exceptionally talented women, like Feinstein, were cherry-picked from these sections to perform more elaborate tasks of deciphering in smaller units.

In late 1939, a good year and a half after her arrival at SIS, Feinstein did the impossible. She managed to crack the Japanese Foreign Office Type-B Cipher Machine, known as "Purple." This machine was an evolution of the previous Japanese cipher machine "Red," which was unreliable and easily broken, while the newer version referenced many of the same Enigma settings from the Germans.

Feinstein sat, head down, pen in hand, engrossed in what was in front of her while fiddling with her spectacles. She looked again, for what seemed like the millionth time, at the same groups of code, but this time around she saw something different. Something new that she hadn't seen before. *Yes! A loophole! A crack! An answer!*

Feinstein had identified the correct pattern that held the whole encryption together, specifically the Romanized Japanese alphabet sequence of code.

She called her supervisors, William Friedman and Frank Rowlett, over to her desk, pointing at something and whispering in their direction. Their eyes widened with amazement and Rowlett exclaimed out loud for everyone to hear, "That's it! That's it! Gene has found what we've been looking for!" (Baraniuk, 2017, para. 16). A round of applause from the team for this bright young lady, who at 27 years of age humbly broke the tough and seemingly impenetrable codes from the Japanese machine.

This would later allow SIS to build an analog machine that would efficiently decrypt the cyclical nature of the code and tap into the diplomatic transmissions between the Japanese high-ranking official Hiroshi Oshima connected to Tokyo and the forces in Berlin.

Feinstein's attitude toward the whole project was clearly reflected in an interview she did in 1991. When asked what kind of feelings she might have towards her success in breaking the Japanese code, she simply said, "Maybe I was just lucky." And when asked about the rotor machine she helped build, she said, "I was excited and interested, looking forward to working on the mechanism. I regarded it more as just one step in a series of steps" (Whitcher Gentzke, 2022, para. 6).

By 1941, the efforts for WWII were underway and the games were in full swing. The more keen ears and sharp eyes on the job, the easier it would be to fish out the right information from the power-crazed Axis leaders.

A year later, President Roosevelt declared the opening of military services to women, in turn creating the new department of Women Accepted for Voluntary Emergency Service (WAVES). Men often referred to women who joined the military as 'petticoat soldiers,' with comments from men often revolving around the sentiment, "This is a man's war. What sort of jobs can they do?"

But the push from the government clearly stated, "It's your war, too!" The 1944 slogan for the short recruitment propaganda in the U.S. targeted the role of servicewomen, expressing that their job was a vitally important support to the war efforts.

This instigated many women to volunteer their services to this branch of the military where they wore a uniform and received officers training, thus becoming full naval officers.

The women enlisted under WAVES were often told very little of their involvement in Naval affairs. Around 600 women and 200 men were sent to Ohio to work on the cryptanalytic machines called Bombes. These Bombes (named after the Polish machine Bomba), were large machines holding 64 rotors that were wired to equally match the rotors used on the Enigma machine.

The women who performed the task of building and applying settings were also then sent out to operate these machines. The issue was that they had no idea what the operation of these machines were for! The men in power chose to keep this a secret from the women, who were thought to be incapable of keeping from gossiping about their work and thus ruining the whole operation.

But this was to become a larger problem when "Commander Gilman McDonnel, a supervisor on the Bombe deck, recalled an incident in which a rotor solution, known as a jackpot, was accidentally thrown out. The resulting delay made it apparent to the chief of the Bombe operations, John Howard, that some kind of explanation was necessary" (Wilcox, 1998, p. 10). This just goes to show how little the men in power trusted the women at keeping a secret or even understanding the magnitude of the operation.

In comparison to the women at WAVES, Feinstein's contribution would be just as clandestine, although even by her own knowledge she too might have been left in the dark on many occasions.

She was now earning quite a bit more money than she had before, but her targets and ciphers were getting a whole lot more complex. This game of cat and mouse was getting tricker by the year.

And to make things a little more distracting for her, during this time she was courted. She met Hyman I. Feinstein in Arlington; a chemist who graduated from Columbia University with Russian heritage. He worked at the National Bureau of Standards as a research assistant and cryptanalyst, and they would often bump into each other around campus.

Another budding love developed in the code rooms. It is hard to decipher the romantic parts of their lives, trying to imagine how they would have behaved towards each other, in comparison to the more open society of today. The norms and standards of the era were so much more reserved and can appear somewhat formal.

Either way, Genevieve and Hyman were married in 1943, maintaining their privacy of each other's work, and rarely, if ever, talking about it openly to each other.

### *Solving Problems*

In that same year, Feinstein was already working on the Soviet problem. Towards the end of WWII and onwards into the Cold War of 1947, Americans were spying on the Russians. This was known as the Venona project, dedicated to picking up and interpreting KGB and Main Intelligence Directorate (GRU) messages which in turn helped high-ranking officials make judgments in the later years of war.

It took the team almost two years to break the KGB code. Feinstein had a brilliant strategy and was critically improving how the method of decoding would evolve and specialize. "She devised a process for recognizing the re-use of key, which, in turn, permitted the decryption of Russian KGB messages" (NSA Genevieve Grotjan, 2022, para. 2). This momentous discovery was then captioned as "the most important single cryptanalytic break in the whole history of Venona" (NSA Genevieve Grotjan, 2022, para. 2).

The Venona code-breaking operation in WWII aimed at the Soviets might seem contradictory, as they were indeed Allies at the time, but there was a level of mistrust that each country had for the other, which required constant monitoring of motivations and actions. Secretly tapping into the Soviet transmissions kept them in check and allowed America to have an upper hand if their fickle friendship turned sour.

The majority of the women within the project were schoolteachers. Gena Grabeel was the founder of the project, and it ran for a good 33 years before being terminated.

The Feinstein couple were soaring! While Genevieve was busy decoding the Soviets, her husband worked on the infamous Manhattan project, involving nuclear weapon research and development. They were both heavily involved in extremely secretive stuff!

Feinstein had a very big year in 1946. At the age of 33, she gave birth to her only son, named Ellis. She would also receive the Exceptional Civilian Award for her great work during the war by going above and beyond her duties. This did not mean that her real work was ever disclosed, only that whatever she was doing, she was doing it very well.

The following year, Feinstein retired from her government work to become a professor of mathematics at George Mason University (GMU) and focus on her family life. Her husband had also taken up a position at the same university teaching chemistry. They were clearly inseparable and more than comfortable working in each other's presence. Their family of three lived in a house in Fairfax, Virginia.

As expected, not much was said in 1945, when Representative Clarence E. Hancock said in the U.S. Congress, "I believe our cryptographers...in the war with Japan did as much to bring to a successful and early conclusion as any other group of men." That is about as much of a public thank you women got for their efforts and sacrifice over the years.

Secrecy, yes. An oath of confidentiality, yes. But why were the men lauded while the women were rendered invisible? Out of the 20,000 American codebreakers, at least 11,000 of them were women.

In 1969, in a very sad turn of events, husband and wife walked downstairs one evening to find their son Ellis dead in the living room. At the age of 22, and with a bright future ahead of him in mathematics, which he was studying at Yale, Ellis died from a severe heart condition.

How utterly crushing for the Feinsteins to lose their only son. Their neighbor of 13 years, Joan Craun, observed that, after the passing of her own son, Genevieve enjoyed spending time with her children and watching them play. She missed being a mother and found ways to give back in tenderness and love through Craun's children, even gifting the daughter her piano.

In 1995, Hyman Feinstein died at the age of 84. Just before his death, he set up the Genevieve Feinstein Award in Cryptography at GMU, which to this day is awarded in honor of outstanding mathematical achievement.

Genevieve Grotjan Feinstein needed in-home care after her husband passed away. She joined him in 2006, passing away peacefully at home at the lengthy age of 93.

## Her Legacy

Genevieve Grotjan Feinstein's exploitation of Japanese and German communication systems was mind-boggling. A real genius in the field that became so popular, thanks to her and other bright stars of the time.

A true reflection of her influence at SIS showed in 1980 when the new department at the NSA elected its new deputy director, Ann Z. Caracristi, a prolific code breaker of Japanese ciphers turned leader.

Feinstein's humble and reserved behavior towards the grueling and arduous work she did when breaking Purple and thousands of other codes was a lovely insight into her personality and demeanor. This gives us the platform to understand that real strength comes from actions, not simply words. This held true even as the years passed, and her world turned upside down after the death of her child.

In 2007, a year after her death, the GMU received a $1 million scholarship program in Ellis' name. And in 2011, she was inducted into the Hall of Honor as the Women of American Cryptology Honoree of the NSA.

Genevieve Feinstein had no living relatives, which sadly meant that when they inducted her posthumously, no one was there to receive the honor for her. Instead, the NSA invited a mathematician from the department GMU.

A sad reminder of the stakes involved in achieving remarkable things. Work was her life, a life that was not seen by many. She took the challenge and sprinted over hurdles, only to disappear into the archives until the late 2000s.

It is high time that quiet, unassuming Genevieve's secret story be told, so that she is not forgotten by history.

# Chapter Four

## Joan Clarke: Hidden Gem

You could call her a plain-looking woman. If she passed you on the street, you might think nothing of her. She would seem like any other office worker, with her hair neatly permed and pinned up, light makeup, simple attire, carrying a standard-issue briefcase.

If you were curious enough to stop her in the streets of London and ask what she did for a living, she would most likely respond with something noncommittal: "Oh, you know. I'm an ordinary pencil pusher for the government," with a shrug of the shoulders and a modest smile. But behind those eyes lay a great secret.

Joan Clarke's achievements are described in a BBC report as:

> "ingenious work as a codebreaker during WWII who saved countless lives, and her talents were formidable enough to command the respect of some of the greatest minds of the 20th Century, despite the sexism of the time."
> 
> (Miller, 2014, para. 1)

Joan Clarke was a woman who was first regarded solely for her relationship with a genius, and then over the years by her own intrinsic relationship with codes.

## Her Early Life

Born in 1917 in the London suburb of West Norwood, Joan Elizabeth Lowther Clarke was the youngest of five children to Reverend William Clarke and his wife Dorothy.

Clarke went to Dulwich High School for Girls for some years before she was awarded a scholarship in 1936 to attend Newnham College in Cambridge and successfully gained the honor of Wrangler in her senior year. A Wrangler is someone who achieves full honors or a double-first in their third year of mathematics. This is impressive indeed.

At 22, Clarke was awarded the Philippa Fawcett prize in 1939, which still today recognizes bright young female mathematicians. This was followed by an acceptance for the Helen Glaston scholarship from 1939 to 1940.

Clarke had some considerable talent, but naturally, she was not permitted to receive her degree, as women were only allowed access to full degrees after 1948. This left her in a state of limbo.

While Clarke was taking an advanced geometry class at Cambridge in 1939, she was noticed by supervisor Gordon Welchman. This man was one of the four cryptanalysts and mathematicians who scouted for young women that could help at Bletchley Park within their Government Code and Cipher School (GCCS).

She was often described as being kind and shy, conforming to her male-dominated arena in a typical and traditional subordinate fashion. The process for recruiting young women into the system required not just talent in sciences and languages, but a certain amount of submissiveness. To fit into this environment, intelligence and determination were key, but so was reserve.

Other women like Clarke would receive letters inviting them to these top-secret meetings where interviews and assessments were done on their talents. The process could take up to a couple of days, making sure they understood both the job and the consequences if something was said or if they were caught. "The work didn't really need mathematics, but mathematicians tended to be good at it" (Lord, 2020, para. 6), thus she accepted the invitation, of course, but only to start working at Bletchley in the following year, 1940, allowing her to finish her master level Part III of the Mathematical Tripos at Cambridge.

This shows us her ideal of working until the job was done! She was not prepared to drop university and go at the command of the men at the top. She was determined to complete the task at hand before moving on to something else. This attitude would reflect clearly in her later work.

*Figure 4: Bletchley Park today*

## Her Career

Bletchley Park was chosen as a location for top-secret cryptologic war departments because of its short distance from Cambridge and Oxford University, where they recruited from among the most brilliant minds of the time. This beautiful building was constructed in the Victorian Gothic, Tudor, and Dutch Baroque styles and was surrounded by large gardens. The plaque at the front gate read: Bletchley Radio Manufacturing. This was a coverup that was not entirely incorrect.

At just 23 years old, Clarke was a budding talent, walking the premises excited and proud. She started working in Hut 8, a building just beside Bletchley, where a large number of women were employed to do all the clerical and analysis work. The women who worked in Hut 8 were referred to as "the girls," which in today's era can strike a sour note and sound rather belittling.

Due to the insufficient space at the premises, the decryption sections were separated into 'Huts' or divisions on the property; Hut 6 was responsible for codebreaking in the German Army and Air Force and Hut 3 was responsible for their translations and processing, while Hut 8 was in charge of deciphering the German Navy codes and Hut 4 was responsible for their translations and processing in turn.

> "Since the focus of each Hut directly related to the job of another Hut, the responsibility of civilians working at Bletchley Park could be specialized, and the information transported by messenger between locations."
>
> (Herndon 2017, p. 7)

Her new life at a top-secret location was doing top-secret work. What on earth would her parents say? *Oh, well. They will never know*, she thought to herself as she entered the premises.

In the first year, she earned a mere £2 a week, working in huge rooms, attached to more huge rooms, filled with desks lined wall to wall. These desks were stationed by young women typing and writing, listening to radio waves through Morse code. Their hair was done up just as fashion dictated at the time, their outfits were formal and plain, spectacles perched on their noses and cigarettes clasped between their red lips.

To file and index, to search and pass on. Information flowed, was destroyed, and flowed again. Ciphers and keys, numbers and letters, signals and waves created transmission after transmission. The women were intercepting these enemy communications, latching on, and decoding. Long hours, little pay.

A woman who worked at Bletchley, Hester Sorel-Cameron, mentions in a later interview how, "Inevitably, the duller routine clerical work was done by women, since only men with what were considered suitable qualification for cryptanalysis or related translation and intelligence work could join in GCCS" (Herndon, 2017, p. 14).

When Clarke's remarkable abilities took the spotlight, she was quickly ushered into Alan Turing's office.

Turing paced up to Clarke, and came straight to the point: "Do you like puzzles, Miss Clarke?" Equally as forthright, she replied, "Yes, I do, Mr. Turing. Very much." Turing looked at her for a long moment and said, "What would you think if I said we can break the Enigma by building an equally fast machine of our own?" She smiled, ready for anything, "That sounds like a tough puzzle, Mr. Turing. When do we start?" Her nervous but eager smile matched his.

## *Stepping Up*

Picture Clarke sitting in a smoky room, filled with papers, machines, and cables. Large chalkboards with scribbles of all kinds on them. "Alan," she would say, softly and calmly, while approaching his desk, "I have been thinking, you know, how my wages are rather inadequate to the current work I am doing for you here at Hut 8." After a long pause, Alan Turing lifted his head up from the pages in front of him, seeming only now to realize that she was speaking to him. He answered with a vague, "Hm-mm" while taking off his spectacles to give them a quick clean. She gingerly sat down on a chair beside him and politely stated, "If I am going to be performing these duties, then I would like an increase. A way to ensure that my worth is recognized, you see." She finally built up the courage to say, "What would you think of me asking for a promotion?"

A bold move to make as a woman in the 1940s; testing her limits and her boundaries, assessing if she could find a loophole in the system.

Clarke was initially classed as a standard administrative clerk and the only way for her to jump the salary bracket was if she changed her class. So, in a clever and quite mischievous application, Turing and the other men in the team were able to help her gain the class of Linguist, which upped her salary considerably. The catch was, she only spoke English.

There was absolutely no position for a senior female cryptanalyst. It simply didn't exist yet. So, in the spirit of a woman of the time, she thoroughly enjoyed filling in her forms with:

*Grade: Linguist. Languages: None.*

We can imagine that she smiled wryly to herself every time she had to scribble it down.

It is important to mention that these codebreakers did not need to know German or Japanese to understand the code (although knowing the language was certainly favorable). The cryptologists would decode number groups directly from cryptography into plaintext and translate them for what *they stood for*. Therefore, the cryptanalysts simply needed to think of the English word for that number group, rather than translate the message into English. The math did the translating for them, as the numerical codes would need to be understood by their frequency analysis.

It is also important to note that naval codes had a very limited vocabulary, which often helped cryptanalysts to quickly pick up the main concept of the message. If they mentioned a certain island, a certain city, or a certain supply ship, then the codebreakers would have learned the key terms in Japanese or German and recognized them immediately.

Linguistic departments, such as the Allied Translator and Interpreter Section (ATIS), also played a key role in shortening the length of the war, thanks to their immediate and efficient translations of Japanese messages. This was a conjoined operation between America and Australia. Many of the people staffed there were Missionaries who had been to the regions and learned the language, as well as half-nationals who spoke a foreign language at home.

So, Clarke, not being a linguist but a proficient mathematician, gained access to one of the most secretive and strategic operations in Great Britain along with a nice increase in pay. She would be working alongside Turing and the other men in the sole pursuit of the German Enigma code. That was the whole reason behind the GCCS operation, as a matter of fact.

## *Breaking the Unbreakable*

We spoke about the uncrackable one-time pad encryption and decipher method earlier in the introduction. Now, it makes sense that this method works well only if the sender and receiver have the exact same pad and know the given key, but if you are planning on sending an unbreakable message across the globe in a far less analog method, then you need something more reliable to encrypt your plans.

*Figure 5: The Enigma encryption machine*

Radio waves and letters sent between Berlin, Tokyo, and the spy rings in enemy nations needed total clearance and privacy. Therefore, the brilliant Enigma machine was developed by the Germans. Like the one-time pad system that used new keys or settings for each message, this electro-mechanic device could spew out an encrypted message that had a different setting every day, thanks to its intricate rotor system.

It looked like a small typewriter, but if you pressed the Y button an S would come out on the paper, then the next day it would be an M, and the following day an F. This leaned the machine an unfathomable complexity, as "chances of being able to decipher a message was an astonishing 150 million to one" (Lord, 2020, para. 3), challenging the Allies for years.

It was considered an impossible undertaking by many, although Alan Turing and the rest of the team certainly didn't think so.

As early as 1932, the Polish mathematician Marian Rejewski already understood the internal mechanisms of the Enigma machine, and in 1938 had built with his team a code-breaking machine called the Bombe, which technically cracked the first phases of the German machine.

In 1939, Nazi Germany invaded Poland, forcing the Polish mathematician to flee the country. He graciously transferred the technology and theory to the British in 1939, and this is how Gordon Welchman and Alan Turing were able to create the Ultra team in Hut 6 that would work closely with the Hut 8 team in the following years. They started building Victoria, one of many different rotor machines that would attempt to decipher German codes instantaneously. It was similar in design to that of Rejewski's prototype, but with a larger spectrum of data analysis.

Clarke had become proficient in the Banburismus analytical process that was developed by Turing. This cryptanalytic process did not require a rotor machine to unscramble like a Bombe, but the rather sequential conditional probability that would 'predict' what the following setting would be on the German Enigma machine. This was the basis for all the machines they built at the time.

At the beginning of 1941, 282,000 tons of shipping were being shot down by the U-boat wolf packs, but by the end of 1941, and all thanks to the immediate and inexhaustible deciphering of Clarke and the rest of the team, they were able to reduce that number to 62,000 tons. "The messages Clarke decoded would result in some military action being taken almost immediately" (Miller, 2014, para. 10), requiring real-time access to all messages and breaking them as fast as humanly possible, something Clarke seemed to be able to do very well.

In the winter of 1942, Turing, Clarke, and the rest of the team broke the Enigma and subsequently built the machine, Tunny, that aided them in intercepting around 39,000 messages in the first month, then gradually increasing until they were decoding around two messages every minute, resulting in something like 84,000 decryptions a month!

The Naval Enigma machine was particularly difficult to crack. When the codebreakers finally cracked it, they had access to the thousands of German U-boat (wolf-packs) messages that signaled where they were, and which Allied supply ships in the Atlantic or Pacific they were targeting. The codebreaking team was equally involved in the preemptive measures when deciphering city strikes, connected to military and naval defense.

When the U.S. code breaking unit OP-20-G stepped in at Bletchley in 1943, many of the Hut 8 staff were transferred to other departments, although Clarke remained put.

In 1944, she earned the role of Deputy Head of Hut 8 where she would continue breaking Dolphin and Shark Naval Enigma messages until the war ended. She never progressed beyond that role at the GCCS. And she was not alone; other codebreakers at Bletchley like Ruth Briggs, Margaret Rock, and Mavis Batey (Chapter 4), all remained under the glass ceiling.

The war was a fresh memory by 1946 and the GCCS operation at Bletchley was dismantled and all evidence removed. Margret Berlin, one of the women who at 18 helped build the Colossus decryption machine in Bletchley Park, stated in an interview with BBC, "I can remember the chap in the office where we worked coming on one day and saying, 'You can go home now, the war is over.' Just like that" (Mulroy, 2019).

Clarke, now 30, along with the team moved to a new division in Eastcote, renamed the Government Communication Headquarters (GCHQ).

The next year, in 1947, Clarke would receive her Member of the British Empire (MBE) for her outstanding work during the war (still utterly top-secret). Here at GCHQ is where she met her future husband Lieutenant John Kenneth Ronald Murray, a colleague of hers and a retired army officer whom she married in 1952.

The similarities in their job and in their personal affairs, like botany and chess, allowed them to connect. Murray was seven years her senior and had some health issues which resulted in them both retiring from the GCHQ shortly after the wedding.

They moved to Scotland, to a small coastal town of Fife, where they would remain for a good 10 years researching Scottish coinage history. She gained an enthusiastic interest in numismatic study (study of ancient coins) thanks to her husband, and together they would write several papers on the subject.

In 1962, the Murrays moved back to England where Clarke resumed her work for the GCHQ until her retirement in 1977.

She was finally able to talk about her past when, in 1974, the seal of the Official Secrets Act was lifted. The activities of Bletchley Park were revealed, and her MBE was recognized by the public.

Her dear husband John died in 1986. Clarke, almost 70, had no intention of slowing down. Moving to a new home near Oxford, she carried on with her study and research into coin history, winning the Sanford Saltus Medal for her contribution to Numismatics. Clarke contributed in 1987 to a book and play by her friend Andrew Hodges on the events of the Enigma code breaking. One of the stage characters was actually based on Clarke.

Then, in 1996, never too far away from her knitting yarn and chessboard, Joan Clarke died at the age of 79 at her home in Headington Quarry near Oxford, with no children to leave behind, but a legacy for all women to uphold.

### *Turing's Friend*

Clarke and Turing became very close during the early 1940s, as they had met each other previously through Clarke's brother. This friendship progressed when Clarke started working at GCCS. When she was eventually placed together with Turing in the core strategic unit, they became fast friends, thanks to their many shared interests.

Clarke epitomizes the relationship she had with Turing in an interview she gave in 1992:

> "I suppose the fact that I was a woman made me different," she says. "We did do some things together, perhaps went to the cinema and so on. But certainly, it was a surprise to me when he said - I think his words were - 'Would you consider marrying me?' But although it was a surprise, I really didn't hesitate in saying yes. And then he knelt by my chair and kissed me. Although we didn't have very much physical contact. Now the next day, I suppose we went for a little walk together after lunch. He told me about this homosexual tendency, and naturally, that worried me a bit, because I didn't know if that was something that was almost certainly permanent. But we carried on."
>
> (Miller, 2014)

Turing obviously loved her as a dear friend, but his affectionate love was directed toward his own sex. Homosexuality was still criminalized, but Clarke seemed unruffled by Turing's revelation that he was gay, perhaps because, as she stated, she was very unsure of what exactly 'homosexual tendencies' really implied for their relationship.

Over their short engagement, Clarke met his parents, and he hers. Turing gave Clarke an engagement ring and they took holidays together. The two of them strictly stipulated that their relationship remain secretive in the workplace, and Clarke never wore her ring at Bletchley. But they eventually broke their engagement, as Turing felt he couldn't live a double life, though they remained close friends for many years after she left the GCCS, corresponding often.

Unfortunately, Turing's sexuality turned society against him when he was discovered with another man in 1953. Turing was rejected and shunned by his department and punished for his 'crime' with forced estrogen injections, also known as chemical castration. Shortly after that, he committed suicide at his house in Wilmslow. He was 41.

A tragic, unjust ending to the story of a man that had given so much to his country, which must have shattered Clarke's heart.

## Her Legacy

Joan Clarke Murray gave many women a reason to step up to the plate. She handled her own within the various departments with poise and equanimity, and just got on with her work. Not too bothered by the restrictions set upon her by society, she was far more interested in growing knowledge and using it for a greater good.

She was a visionary, as was her friend and tutor, Turing. Their differences were what connected them in the first place as many of these women were considered outliers to begin with.

Being "a clever woman" was not often a compliment at this point in history. In theory, it is possible that the Bletchley women enjoyed more understanding and consideration within their secretive workplaces than in society at large, in the hope that men at Bletchley Park appreciated them for their intelligence, which usually had to be disguised in the world outside its gates.

Winning the war was their main priority and through it all, they also won friendships and love along the way too.

*The Imitation Game* is a movie released in 2014 that broadly depicts the circumstances and struggles of WWII, specifically within the successes and failures of the cryptology team at Bletchley Park. It is worth noting that the roles of historical female figures are, more often than not, written by men. And while the theme of the movie was centered on Alan Turing's work—portrayed by actor Benedict Cumberbatch—it can be argued that the role of Joan Clarke's character, portrayed by actor Keira Knightley, as fundamental in the life of the team, was not given sufficient credit.

As better and truer representations of female roles come to our screens, we can but hope that we will soon see a film dedicated to the women code breakers of WWII.

# Chapter Five

## Mavis Batey: Codebreaking Landscaper

Mavis Lilian Lever Batey's love for different facets of life is quite intriguing. Her mind, equally proficient at linguistics as it was at deciphering codes, culminates later in her interpretation of historical gardens.

A calm and resourceful woman, like Joan Clarke who worked in the opposite building at Bletchley Park, Batey's natural recognition of patterns created meaning where others saw only the random or the absurd.

This enigmatic British code breaker's humble take on her own wartime experiences makes her story all the more curious and intriguing - a mystery yet to be fully unraveled.

### Her Early Life

Mavis Lilian Lever was born in 1921, in the South London suburb of Dulwich. Her father was a postman, her mother a seamstress, and their middle-class family values were emphasized to their daughter, which later fueled her interest in looking beyond the horizon.

When she was young, the family moved to Norbury, where she attended an all-girls school in Croydon called Coloma Convent. She evidently had a passion for languages, as she eagerly asked her parents if she could go to Germany on holiday as a present for passing her German O Level.

She relished the romances of the country, in the literature and poetry of Germanic history. Hence, when she returned to Great Britain in 1939, she decided to take German Literature classes at University College London.

But alas, as of September that year, WWII broke out. She saw the world starting to panic and the news getting bleaker by the day. Batey mentioned in one of her interviews:

> "I didn't want to go on with academic studies. University College was just evacuating to the campus at Aberystwyth, in West Wales. But I thought I ought to do something better for the war effort than reading German poets in Wales. After all, German poets would soon be above us in bombers. It was remarked by someone that I should train to be a nurse."
>
> (Simkin, 2020)

The 18-year-old Batey pondered what she should do now that everything she knew was turning upside down. Her college friend approached her saying, "Mavis, you are so brilliant at German, why not use that to your advantage? They are calling out for linguists, you know." Mavis looked out of her college window thinking deeply about her future, "Well, I suppose," she mused, "it wouldn't be the worst idea, although someone mentioned to me recently that I should perhaps become a nurse and join the Red Cross. I simply don't know if that is something I would be good at."

She would find her niche sooner than she thought.

### *More Than Just a Language*

Mari K. Eder's 2020 book *The Girls Who Stepped Out of Line* details well the perspectives of the time. Eder writes that "Hiring women during World War II was a difficult and unwelcome chore for many male managers." Already, 11% of the population was being shipped out to warring zones, but things still had to keep running and operations needed manning. So, "while the men were away at war, women needed to save the home front and the economy at the same time. An act of bravery. Prepared or not, they took up the challenge" (Eder, 2020, p. 3). And many of these women did. Many for the first time in their lives.

This recruitment of women was especially true in areas of code-breaking and translation. This was an immensely delicate and secretive task, which meant complete and utter loyalty. If even one of these codebreakers broke their silence or turned Axis spy, the outcome of WWII might have been vastly different. The British and American governments recruited half-Japanese and half-German civilians to assist in the translation and interpretation of war efforts. They were often given the Test of Loyalty Questionnaire, which consisted of a set of 28 questions regarding their family history and their allegiance to their original country of nationality (if they were half-nationals, that is).

So, in the following months of 1939, Batey was recruited to the Ministry of Economic Warfare in London, whose involvement in the war was through espionage, reconnaissance, and sabotage. Thanks to her advantageous knowledge of the German language, she would quickly be indispensable. Her job was to sort through the personal columns of *The Times* newspapers for possible coded messages while also blacklisting nationals who were still dealing with anyone from the Axis powers. This must have been a very tiresome job to do, going through lists all day long.

Many women were considered better suited for tedious time-consuming work, like administration, translation, and intercepting codes. Ann Caracristi, the American codebreaker, once said, "It was generally believed that women were good at doing tedious work, and as I had discovered early on, the initial stages of cryptanalysis were very tedious, indeed" (Mundy, 2017, para. 14). Women were limited to serving men higher up in the hierarchy exactly what they needed. Other STEM fields, like mathematics and astronomy, saw the same pattern occur; where women were relegated to being "paper pushers or "calculators" while the button pushers were men.

The now 19-year-old Batey must have believed this was all very odd and highly exciting, even though, just as all the other women before and after her, she did not know what her actual job would entail. She recalls how her earlier interpretation of being a spy was "seducing Prussian officers." Imagine her surprise when she "found herself ensconced in what had been a laborer's cottage in Bletchley Park, breaking codes and changing the course of the Second World War" (McSmith, 2008, para. 2).

Batey was soon spotted by a Bletchley Park recruiter after showing signs of not only being good at translating efficiently, but also recognizing secret patterns within these languages. Consequently, she was picked for training at the GCCS at Bletchley Park in Buckinghamshire. When Batey was told that the work being done at Bletchley was top secret, that she was about to learn something great, and that this skill would help end the war and bring the US soldiers and Allied forces home quicker than expected, how could she deny the call?

## Her Career

Her career as a life-saving code breaker really began when she stepped foot in Bletchley Park. You might be wondering how a linguist, who never studied mathematics or cryptology, would begin to enjoy or remotely understand the concept of codebreaking. But that is a rather important point, because cryptography and linguistics *are actually related* by way of information theory. Cryptology is concerned with communication redundancy (remove and modify the message), while linguistics is involved in the structure of signals in a language. There was a similarity in how a language could be molded into another.

That is why many of the recruitment stages in Bletchley history revolved around crosswords. If a person could break a crossword, which is a battle between the setter and the solver, in an allotted space of time, then they were better for the job than most. The battle of wits and lateral thinking was afoot and as Alan Turing said himself: "It was problem solvers they needed; unconventional thinkers to solve the problem" (Chivers, 2014, para. 8).

## *A Fast Learner*

Batey quickly understood the concepts in her code classes at GCCS in 1940. She showed great promise when she spotted an interesting Morse code transmission under STGOCH. While many wondered if there could be a saint called Goch, a Batey saw through the ruse and was successfully able to decode the transmission as Santiago, the now capital of Chile.

When training was complete, she was initially stationed in N°3 Cottage, a research division targeting fresh encrypted messages every day with women passing them along the paper trail. She was quickly scouted once more and moved to Hut 6 as assistant to the eccentric and brilliant mind of Alfred Dilwyn (Dilly) Knox.

Knox had already gained fame during WWI for decoding the Zimmerman Telegram, and had built a good team at the facility since then. Author Sinclair McKay, in his 2011 historical book *The Secret Life of Bletchley Park*, regards Knox's varied ideas about women saying, "Dilwyn Knox… found that women had a greater aptitude for the work required, as well as nimbleness of mind and capacity for lateral thought, they possessed a care and attention to detail than many men might not have had" (Simkin, 2020b, para. 9). McKay also remarks that a possible reason for employing so many young women was because he just didn't like men that much. Many commented that he would often be found sleeping in his office for days on end trying to solve cipher problems.

Knox was said to be a great teacher, constantly asking his assistants to "look at problems from unexpected angles" (Simkin, 2020b, para. 11), and he was sure that if all codebreakers were mathematicians, it would cause problems, as he believed that mathematicians could be very unimaginative.

Years later, in an interview with McKay, Batey shines a light on her initial ignorance of the complex Enigma machine which she would eventually help decipher, stating:

> "We were all thrown in the deep end. No one knew how the blessed thing worked. When I first arrived, I was told, 'We are breaking machines, have you got a pencil?' And that was it. You got no explanation. I never saw an Enigma machine. Dilly Knox was able to reduce it, I won't say to a game, but sort of a linguistic puzzle. It was rather like driving a car while having no idea what goes on under the bonnet."
> (Simkin, 2020a, para. 9)

Batey found herself working under Knox's wing between 1940 and 1941 helping him decode the Italian Enigma Machine. Knox was so impressed by Batey's sheer hard work that he praised her efforts to the Foreign Office in 1940, stating "Miss Lever [Batey] is the most capable and the most useful and if there is any scheme of selection for a small advancement in wages, her name should be considered" (Simkin, 2020b, para. 9).

Along with a friend and colleague, Margaret Rock, Batey became familiar with the style of each Italian Enigma operator and had "worked out that two of the Enigma machine operators had girlfriends called Rosa and as she worked it out, trying different options, like crosswords, it was an obvious option elsewhere" (Chivers, 2014, para. 7). She was quickly connecting the dots and was able to now decode their main sequences, she just needed a hint of a key.

Then, on a day like any other, while intercepting messages between Italian high commanders, something interesting caught Batey's eye. The Enigma message she deciphered read, "Today's the day minus three."

*Well, that is most odd,* she thought to herself. Perplexed at this arbitrary statement, she cracked down for three days on the messages that come next, combing and analyzing their intentions. Finally, she managed to decipher the Italian Navy's Enigma code that would reveal their devious plan to ambush the Royal Navy supply ships between Egypt and Greece. But it had already been three days since that message arrived! So she needed to be fast at alerting the fleet.

Batey's immediate notification to the commanding officers gave the Royal Navy, specifically Admiral Andrew Cunningham, the opportunity to intercept and defeat the Italian fleet before they could attack their supply ships in Cairo: "Cunningham's ships sank three heavy cruisers and two destroyers with the loss of 3,000 Italian soldiers. The Italian fleet never confronted the Royal Navy again" (Smith, 2013, para. 3).

This was to be known as the Battle of Matapan, and in the effort to keep Bletchley's secret of cracking the Italian Enigma code to themselves, the Air Force pretended that it had 'randomly spotted' the Italian ships on the Mediterranean while doing reconnaissance. Very smart move!

Dilly Knox, being an avid poet, and amazed by his assistant's encouraging work, wrote a tribute: "When Cunningham won at Matapan, By the grace of God and Mavis, *Nigro simillima cygno est*, praise Heaven, A very *rara avis*" (Smith, 2013, para. 5). Translating to, "like the black swan, she is, praise Heaven, a very rare bird."

Batey was clearly exceptional and dedicated to the cause, because she had accomplished all of this before her 20th birthday!

### *Feeding the Nazis Fallacies*

As WWII stretched on, so did Mavis Batey's experience at Bletchley. Along with Dilly Knox and Margaret Rock, the team set their sights on a new target; the German Abwehr (German military intelligence unit) Enigma machine transmitting incredibly valuable military intelligence between Berlin and Belgrade. If the team got a chance to infiltrate this communication, they could change the outcome of the war.

By breaking one of the messages along that crucial link, Batey and the team were able to reconstruct one of the Enigma rotors, and from there, the Abwehr Enigma started to reveal itself.

Their code-breaking team was a part of a bigger operation, known as the Double-Cross System, run as the XX-Committee. Led by John Masterman, this operation "would attempt to turn German agents against their masters and persuade them to cooperate in sending false information back to Berlin" (Simkin, 2020b, para. 14).

Through Batey and the rest of the team's decryption of those crucial messages between diplomats, it was found that the Axis command was very gullible indeed, believing the Double-Cross intelligence information being fed to them. This would eventually give the Allies the upper hand in winning the war in 1944 through their false ETA at Normandy Beach on D-Day. The Germans were not present in sufficient numbers to defend the French coast, thanks to the ruse, leaving way for the Allies to commence the largest seaborne invasion in history.

During the four years of war, Batey worked beside a lot of men, and one of them was the mathematician and senior codebreaker, Keith Batey. They spent hours with each other trying to come up with solutions to mind-boggling problems. This, as you may have already begun to suspect by now, led them to fall in love, and they married in 1942.

Many courtships and marriages developed from the interactions in secret code-breaking rooms, especially in the atmospheric years of war. While all staff were expected to always keep the rule of utter confidentiality and secrecy surrounding their work, that did not mean that they could not pursue romantic relationships.

Batey remarked in an interview with the *Independent* about the hardships of keeping secrets from the family saying, "Actually, I was lucky, because I married a mathematician from Hut 6, so although we never talked to the family or anyone else, we have talked about it to each other" (McSmith, 2008, para. 5).

The war came to an end in 1945 and Batey and their three children, Christopher, Deborah, and Elizabeth, decided to move to Canada while Keith finished his Fleet Air Arm flying course. They lived there until 1955 before returning to Great Britain to live in the town of Farnham in the county of Surrey.

## *Patterns in Gardens*

Mavis Batey, at the age of 34, was becoming rather curious about landscaping and the architectural and mathematical concept of gardening. She found this inspiration from W. G. Hoskin's historical writings on the English landscape and her own husband's mathematical comments on the subject. She started to build an idea around the practice of gardening with historical context.

When her husband was appointed to Oxford University as the secretary of the chest (Chief Financial Officer in today's terms) in the 1960s, the whole family moved into the historical grounds of the university.

You can imagine her delight walking through those ancient and historical gardens of Nuneham Park, which sparked her interest in researching landscaping projects.

Batey believed that there was not enough recognition or respect for the gardens in southern England. She wanted her voice to be heard and "she became an immensely inspirational force behind moves by the Garden History Society, Campaign to Protect Rural England, and English Heritage to protect them" (Smith, 2013, para. 14).

Thanks to her dedication, she became the honorary secretary at the Garden History Society in 1971, moving up to honorary president before retiring from the position in 1985.

That very year, Batey received the Veitch Memorial Medal by the Royal Horticultural Society honoring her dedication, and a few years later became an MBE (Member of the British Empire award) for conservation efforts in historic gardens.

Her absolute fascination with the patterns within landscaping would develop further, allowing her to author no less than six books on landscaping in history and fiction during the '90s.

In 2009, she wrote a touching biography on Dilly Knox titled *Dilly: The Man Who Broke Enigmas,* which lovingly depicts a mentor and friend to Batey.

She says in an interview with McKay:

> "I didn't really get back into any kind of intellectual activity until my three children were grown. After that, I could go to the Bodleian Library every day, eventually picking up."
> (Simkin, 2020b, para. 20)

In 2010, Batey became a widow. Just a few months before her death in 2013, she completed her grand finale project, which was to inspire an American Garden Trail at Bletchley Park, that would be populated with flowers and trees from each state of the U.S.A.

Her life had come full circle and all strands of the patterns of her life's work were drawn together, combining her two careers to create a legacy of peace and beauty in the top-secret code-breaking world of Bletchley Park, which had played such a significant part in the war.

## Her Legacy

In a later interview with McKay for his book, Batey wondered, "When you think that about nine or ten thousand people worked in all the various sections of Bletchley Park," she adds, "it is really quite incredible that the secret never got out. Imagine so many people keeping such a secret now" (McKay, 2011, p. 6).

Each year, a competition is set up in order to honor Mavis Batey's life and achievements. Since 2005, The Mavis Batey Essay Prize has been held at The Garden Trust and brings together international university students and graduates to compete and bring forth new and exciting research and writing on gardening and landscaping.

Batey's life is an inspiration in the art of following a passion. From early linguistic and poetic inspirations, she became a secret code breaker during the war, and when the world went back to normal, she found landscape gardening.

Despite her incredible achievements during the war, her modesty was admirable. She never made much of a fuss about it. Five years before her death, in 2008, Batey did an interview with the *Independent* newspaper, where she resolutely played down her contribution. "I must absolutely emphasize that I take absolutely no credit for this [helping end the war]. I was the one who happened to get the message to decode" (McSmith, 2008).

# CHAPTER SIX

## FLORENCE VIOLET MCKENZIE: NONE LIKE MRS. MAC

*Figure 6: Florence Violet McKenzie in WESC uniform*

The first female electrical engineer in Australia, who helped train many hundreds of women and men in Morse code during the war, was known for her determination in settings dominated by men.

Florence Violet McKenzie was a small woman, no more than five feet tall. She was described as "dainty and essentially feminine with her friendly and unassuming manner" (Nelms, 2012, para. 7), but her diminutive stature contrasted vividly with her incredible determination and refusal to be cowed.

Author David Dufty, who wrote a biography on McKenzie in 2020 titled *Radio Girl: The story of the extraordinary Mrs. Mac, pioneering engineer and wartime legend* explains in an interview with Australian podcast show host Michael McLaren: "Well she was quite well-known during and immediately after the war, but her reputation faded over time, and she's one of those people who sort of fall through the cracks of history" (McLaren, 2021).

Violet McKenzie's contributions to science and engineering, women's rights, and education started long before the arrival of WWII.

Australia was monumental in helping the war efforts in WWII, therefore this chapter and the next addresses the role played by the female heroes that were born and bred into a country that was not ready for war, but that made its impact nonetheless.

## Her Early Life

Florence Violet Wallace McKenzie was born in Melbourne, Australia, in 1890. Her father, James Granville (parentage still under question), was reportedly a miner who died when she was just a few years old. Her mother, Marie Anne, remarried in 1894 to a salesman and former miner, George Wallace. Young Violet (which she preferred to be called) and her older brother Walter took his surname.

She and her brother were enthralled by wiring and electrical circuits from a young age, fascinating their parents with all their tinkering and experimentation. They set up torches and connected bells and buzzers to everything, probably with the use of their father's tools and guidance. McKenzie implicitly understood the mechanics of electricity and the potential of wiring connections.

The family moved from a small town called Hawthorne in Victoria to a town south of Sydney called Austinmer. There, McKenzie attended Thirroul School until she was accepted to go to Sydney Girls High School on bursary after showing a high aptitude for mathematics. She completed her academics at high school in 1909 and began setting her sights on a career in the sciences.

## *A First*

In 1915, at the age of 25, McKenzie started studying science at the University of Sydney, passing both Geology and Chemistry but not finishing, because she was unable to take all the other foundational classes that were necessary for her to gain access to the Electrical Engineering department at the university. But that would not stop her.

She did a brief period of teaching mathematics at Armidale High before deciding to focus on her engineering at full throttle. Her brother Walter had just returned from England after finishing his degree in electrical engineering, which inspired her next move. In 1922, she won her diploma in electrical engineering at Sydney Technical College in Ultimo, NSW, and graduated in 1923.

McKenzie was the first woman to receive a diploma in Australia and the first female electrical engineer too! She later donated her diploma to the Ultimo Powerhouse Museum of Historical Records.

With characteristic tenacity, she managed to convince the men at the College to allow her to enroll. In an interview done in 1979 at her nursing home, McKenzie recalls:

> "I went down to Technical College and saw the Head there, and he said, 'Oh, you can't come here and do engineering unless you're working at it'…I said, 'Well now, suppose I had an electrical engineering business and I'm working at it, would that be all right?' He said, 'Yes if you produce proof.' So I went back and I had some cards printed with my name on, and electrical work, and got the paper and wrote down the ads, and read that a house… way out beyond Marrickville somewhere, was asking for prices for putting in electric light and power… I went out there and nobody else was silly enough to go, so they gave me the job. It was about a mile from the end of the tram line… I went back to Tech and took my card down and showed them the contract for the job, and they said, 'All right, you can start'."
>
> (Freyne, 2018, para. 6)

She worked throughout her academic career as a contractor, even buying her own radio and repair shop in Sydney called The Wireless Shop. She said that when schoolboys visited her shop, they would chat to her about a new system of telecommunication which piqued her attention significantly, greatly complimenting her interest in novel ways of communication.

"G'day Miss Wallace," a young boy would say as he entered her shop to collect a piece of equipment. "Have you seen this gadget called a Morse key? Watch me do Morse code on it!" She would smile, quickly peering up from behind her thick-rimmed spectacles while behind the front desk. "Morse code?" she replied quizzically, still fiddling with something on the counter. "Yeah, a set of dots and dashes that encode a message. It's fair dinkum!

Morse code was a quick and efficient way of communicating over long distances, invented by an American team led by Samuel Morse in the 1830s. A specific combination of dots and dashes, also called dits and dahs, each signifying a letter of the alphabet or a number from 0 to 9, which is in fact a general-use cryptographic system in itself.

McKenzie was curious and determined to understand this concept. The schoolboys in her shop showed her how it worked. If it was going to change the world, then she needed to be a part of it!

*Figure 7: Three members of the Women's Emergency Signaling Corps gathered around a radio.*

## Her Career

The following year, in 1924, at the age of 34, McKenzie became the first female certified radio-telegraphist (telegraphy being the long-distance transmission of communication by electric signals running through wires), and the first female member of the Wireless Institute of Australia (an amateur radio society). And of course, she was the first woman to hold an amateur wireless license in the country. What this really meant was that she was now able to legally transmit messages via radio waves, her calling sign was known as VK2FV.

A telegraphist or telegrapher is a person who operates the telegraph machine. They listen in with headphones at Morse code signals and write them down then send back Morse code information using the telegraph key (the contraption they press with their finger). These systems initially used wiring, and land cables that run miles and miles to another destination, but with the invention of the radio and wireless communication, things started getting interesting!

Little did McKenzie know then that her obsessive involvement in communication technology would sweep her off her feet. By 1941, she started to see the true calling of her career and she grabbed it with both hands.

### *Plugging In*

Towards the end of 1924, while McKenzie was still running her radio shop, she was invited to travel to the U.S. for business where she also did an interview with American radio station 6 KGO in San Francisco.

*Figure 8: Old Morse code booklet*

"Miss Wallace, an electrical engineer from Australia, will now talk from the studio," announces the radio presenter. Apparently, from then the interview centered on one thing and one thing only; she "reportedly used her time on air to comment on the difference between the tram system in San Francisco and those in Sydney" (Freyne, 2018, para. 10). A very small percentage of that radio time was spent discussing radio and her accomplishments.

In the U.S., she watched television for the first time in her life, excited about the field of science and experimenting often with television engineering. She believed that chemistry was a solution to improving television and her experiments were noteworthy.

When she returned to Sydney, not too long after that, she married her longtime boyfriend Cecil McKenzie on New Year's Eve, whom she had met through her shop sometime before. Cecil was also an electrical engineer and worked for the Sydney County Council's Electricity Undertaking. They bonded over their shared passion for engineering and radio, and after they tied the knot, they built a house together in Greenwich. This house was a marvel of engineering with fully electric wiring all around and a room that was entirely wireless.

Another mutual fascination the couple had was the study of tropical fish, especially in water heating and salt composition of tanks. In their front yard in Greenwich was a huge fishpond with a variety of species along with aquatic plants. McKenzie did some talks on the radio about her study and published articles in the Australian journal *Aquariana*.

McKenzie must have enjoyed a wry sense of humor. She recalls that one day she was busy doing some contract work at a restaurant, rewiring and "hammering away" (Freyne, 2018, para. 11) when the manager came up to her and said, "Hey, Missy, will you stop that for a minute." She replied, "Yes, I'm sorry. What's the trouble?" Ironically, he said, "I want to listen to the session coming on, about tropical fish." Which of course, was her session she had done a few days earlier for Radio 2FC.

McKenzie founded the Electrical Association of Women (EAW) in 1934 which would teach women how to use electrical equipment safely as she saw the potential of training her customers and sharing information in lectures.

This became a great priority to her when tragedy struck her life that very year. It was early morning, and she was bending down to collect her daily newspaper when she found her neighbor's 13-year-old son dead in her front yard. The autopsy revealed that he had died of electrocution. The report stated that the boy's playing with a switch outside her house that lit up the grounds and then accidentally touching a live wire while standing in a puddle of rain had been enough to kill him.

To make matters worse, the boy's father had made arrangements to fly from a remote mining station in Western Australia to Greenwich for the funeral but, tragically, died the very next day when the plane crashed. On the third day, a double funeral took place, for father and son.

What a cruel twist of fate that a boy should die from electrocution at the house of a couple of famous electrical engineers. This tragic incident had a profound impact on the McKenzies.

Over the years, some pointed towards a lack of earthing on the switch, some to a lack of maintenance by husband and wife, and others as just foul luck. They were not deemed culpable for the accident and the McKenzies never spoke about it, even if the subject was broached.

Two years later, she wrote and published her EAW Cookery Book which aimed at guiding women in cooking and cleaning with electric appliances safely. She also published various other articles on the proper safe usage of electricity which included children's educational books on the matter, understandably, and did talks about the dangers of electrocution and the correct processes of resuscitation thereafter.

McKenzie wanted to spare women domestic imprisonment by highlighting faster and easier ways to cook and clean. She wrote in a journal in 1935, "To see every woman emancipated from the 'heavy' work of the household by the aid of electricity is in itself a worthy object" (Freyne, 2018, para. 28).

The McKenzies had tried to have a baby two years into their marriage, but sadly it was stillborn. From there, they chose to not have children and were quite happy to sometimes take care of her older brother's two sons, Merton and Lindsay, who would later open up their own radio shop in Melbourne.

So, with the time to focus on her career and her passions, McKenzie closed her wireless shop in Sydney in 1936 to remodel her world around training others.

In 1938 she joined the Australian Women's Flying Club as secretary, and there began training female pilots in the art of Morse code. A futurist for sure, because McKenzie foresaw the war stripping the country of men and leaving critical space in telecommunications open. Consequently, she began the Women's Emergency Signaling Corps (WESC) with the help of her husband in 1939, to train hundreds of future female wireless telegraphists at no charge.

This free service tuition is something that today we are largely unaware of. During the war, efforts towards helping your country often came with minimal or no reward, many companies and organizations concentrated their force on volunteer work alone. And that is how Violet McKenzie grasped her audience of women, because she trained them for the sake of her country, not for her financial gain, believing in them and acknowledging their value.

In a later interview with *Australian Women's Weekly,* she said, "When Neville Chamberlain came back from Munich and said, 'Peace in our time', I began preparing for war" (Freyne, 2018, para. 36). This speech by the British Prime Minister in 1938 upon his return to Britain from a meeting with Hitler was bitterly ironic, as the promise of peace between the two nations turned into outright war one year later.

Within six months, WESC (also known as 'Sigs') was training over 150 women in signaling and Morse code and by the middle of 1940, the school had a waiting list of 600 women. The signaling school operated without a government grant and instead received a single shilling (equivalent to 5 pence or 8 cents) donations each week by the women who trained there to help with the rent.

Many women in her class struggled to comprehend the teachings of Morse code, as they had to memorize all these signals by heart and would confuse the 'dits' (dots) with the 'dahs' (dashes). So she came up with a fun mnemonic for difficult letters and numbers and made clever rhymes to the sounds in Morse codes of each letter and number. For instance, the letter L stood for 'dit-dah-dit-dit' which she would quickly replace with 'to hell with it,' (the word hell sounding like L), or B stood for 'dah-dit-dit-dit' which she associated with 'beef sausages' (B for beef). This method of association allowed the women to learn in half the time and with twice as much fun.

Then, of course, in 1939 the famous broadcast across Australia by PM Robert Menzies somberly read:

> "Fellow Australians, it is my melancholy duty to inform you officially that of consequence from a persistence by Germany in her invasion of Poland, Great Britain has declared war upon her. And as a result, Australia is also at war."
> (Wartime broadcast, 2017).

Even though Australia became a self-governing domain under the British Empire in 1901, Britain still had strong ties to foreign policy, immigration, and the economy. During WWII, the governing system went into *de facto* mode. This means that the Australian government gave Britain the ability to make legally valid actions without actually being the legal authority to do so. In simpler terms: Australia let Britain take the reins and help them defend and fight the war. Therefore, Australia pooled forces in the Pacific theater against Japan and also sent troops out to North Africa, Europe, and the Mediterranean.

At this time, McKenzie had already trained almost 3,000 women on signaling courses and Morse code. The Australian government set out to create the Special Intelligence Bureau in Melbourne's Victoria Barracks (later known as FRUMEL) as a specialized code breaking unit during the war.

The Australian Navy requested that McKenzie's 'girls' be ready to staff this new facility as the war started. These female telegraphists needed to learn Japanese naval codes and by the end of 1941, their unit had expanded considerably.

But what was she to do for all the men that enlisted and needed to know this skill as well?

## *Pushing Back*

A man walked past the WESC school on Clarence street in Sydney and heard the typical beeps of Morse code sounding out over the street. He walked into the premises. McKenzie was called over to the reception, "Mrs. Mac!" one of the ladies called out to her affectionately by her nickname, "There is a gentleman here with a question for you." McKenzie walked out of the noisy room filled with women and into the reception where she was surprised as well as relieved to hear these words come out of the gentleman's mouth, "Will you teach me Morse code?" (Freyne, 2018, para. 42).

*Of course! This was it.* She couldn't just focus on women's training, and she couldn't teach the men at Sigs because it was strictly a women-only school, so she needed another plan. She needed to use them to train other men! Train women to train men. *Perfect.*

Many men who wanted to join the Air Force or the Navy needed to know Morse code before they were allowed to enlist. This was a new thing, a novel request, meaning that thousands of soldiers and countrymen needed her training in a hurry.

Therefore, she began instructor courses for the women, who would then in turn train the men in larger classes at their facility. This became so popular that they had to expand the premises from their 9 Clarence Street address as well as purchase property on the other side of the road, which happened to be a three-story woolshed that needed renovation. After all, this was the only school in Sydney teaching Morse code, and people were streaming in.

In later years, McKenzie talked about the 12,000 recruits and servicemen who passed through WESC during the entire war, mentioning how she saw the likes of Royal Australian Air Force (RAAF) soldiers, The Royal Indian Navy, countless American soldiers, and a good number of police officers training before enlisting in the Air Force. It was a sensation, and the women that McKenzie had trained were very good at their jobs.

*Figure 9: Three women in WESC uniforms. Left to right: Mrs Florence Violet McKenzie, founder of WESC; Pat McInnes; Esme Kura Murrell*

Biographer David Dufty writes in his book *Radio Girls* how immensely proud she was of her "Girls in Green" (as she had sewn outfits for the instructors of WESC) and how the later arrival of male troops also brought respect for her authority. She was able to teach the officers of the U.S. Navy the same way she taught her girls years earlier, but instead of made-up rhymes, this time she used children's music as a platform to remember the semaphore (flag communication systems) patterns. Picture all these rugged navy men waving their flags and singing 'The Teddy Bears Picnic' in class! Priceless view for any woman in that room.

In 1941, the wife of the New South Wales governor, Margaret Wakehurst, paid a visit to the 'Sigs' and mentioned that McKenzie had done "more than any other woman in her contribution to Australia's war effort" (Rees, 2020, para. 28). But that was not the peak for McKenzie. Not yet.

She knew that she needed to do more. It was not enough just to teach the skill; she wanted her girls *in the skill* working as telegraphists in the Air Force and Navy. It made logical sense and it would save precious time, as her students were extremely capable and in high demand.

Predictably, there was some considerable pushback from authoritative positions. This was clearly demonstrated when she wrote a letter in 1940 to Billy Hughes, the Minister of the Navy saying, "I would like to offer the services of our Signaling Corps, if not acceptable as telegraphists, then at least as instructors" (Freyne, 2018, para. 42).

This request would be utterly dismissed. She would try to call the Sydney Naval command and simply receive a "Women in the Navy?" followed by roaring laughter, "Never!" (Dufty, 2020, p. 97). She often found scorn being poured on her novel techniques and methods in Morse code training, until she boarded a train to Melbourne, Victoria, to speak to the Navy Board in person.

Only then did one of the Navy Board members consider coming around to WESC in Sydney and confirming if "her girls" were as reliable and cooperative as she said. Director of Signals and Communications, Commander Newman, would find that these women were indeed very proficient at signaling and after a bit more convincing to HQ, and the obvious urgent need for telegraphists, the Navy eventually agreed, although with a fair degree of skepticism.

*Figure 10: Group portrait of WRANS and two sailors on staff at HMAS Harman*

Thus, in April of 1941, women were officially allowed entry into the Navy. Initially, only 14 trained women were accepted into the force from the WESC school. This would eventually become the core unit and seed of the Women's Royal Australian Naval Service (WRANS). These women would be initially stationed at the naval base HMAS Harman.

The Royal Australian Air Force (RAAF) established the Women's Auxiliary Australian Air Force (WAAAF) which worked closely with the WRANS, and where McKenzie became an honorary flight officer, meaning that she could now legally teach Air Force students.

By the end of the war, the WRANS had expanded considerably, filling out at least 2,600 positions, which was then a good 10% of the entire Naval force. Sigs branches were popping up in the other cities of Brisbane, Inverell, Wagga Wagga, and Taree.

Many men were nipping at her heels now as McKenzie had garnered too much fame; she was everywhere on the news and people all over the world knew about her name. So of course, around this time she would also receive some sour comments on her vision.

General Thomas Blamey spoke out in 1941 against the signaling movement saying, "not a bit of use, women training to be dispatch riders and signallers or doing any military things" (Rees, 2020, para. 1).

She told the press how she felt, retorting energetically:

> "I am writing General Blamey a letter to explain the work our organization is doing. By his statement on the uselessness of women training to be signallers, I am convinced he has no knowledge whatsoever of the work which the Women's Emergency Signaling Corps are doing."
>
> (Dufty, 2020, p. 129)

She definitely was a different kind of woman at that time. She stuck to her principles and knew how to use publicity to her advantage to make a point. She rarely let men get away with questioning her judgment.

In 1958, McKenzie was awarded the first-class category aircrew license which was a revised certification for a Flight Radio Telephony Operators License. To receive this license required the person to have accumulated 50 hours of flying, which of course, women were never seen doing then. How she was able to log the hours and get the training is still not confirmed and is a mystery. This was discovered thanks to a journalist finding the aircrew certificate many years later.

But it is important to note that the first woman to receive the qualification of telephony operator was one of McKenzie's own students at WRANS, a certain Patricia Whyte, who received the success for her accomplishment while McKenzie was never mentioned.

Even once the war had died down, her school kept on teaching voluntary civilian and Navy personnel while never actually receiving an official status. As long as there was a need for wireless signaling training, then her school would help. She was praised in a statement made by Captain Pearson, principal of the Richmond Nautical School in Sydney, in 1948: "Mrs. McKenzie is worthy of the highest honor Australia can bestow. All who can help to advance this recognition are invited to contact us. This is not an appeal for funds, but for support in placing the fact in the right place for appropriate recognition" (Dufty, 2020, p. 142). McKenzie, as a woman, could not get a knighthood, but she was appointed the Order of the British Empire (OBE) in 1950 for her voluntary services.

Many Air Force pilots were moving from the military services into commercial flying through Australian National Airlines (now Qantas); therefore, the department equipped WESC premises with all the necessary radio equipment so that her instructors could teach these pilots specific courses on how to use the modem and signal Morse at a faster pace. So, by 1952, WESC had trained 1050 seamen and 2450 pilots in signaling courses that earned them the necessary 'signaling ticket' to enter the department of Civil Aviation and merchant fleets.

In an ironic turn of events in 1952, led by the Australian National Airlines, McKenzie's lease on the woolshed premises opposite WESC was suddenly terminated by the airline company. She was unceremoniously requested to evict with a letter sent out to, "FV McKenzie (*a female*) 10 Clarence Street, Sydney" (Dufty, 2020, p. 93).

She let her situation be known to a journalist at the *Sydney Morning Herald*, who protested on her behalf. The public embarrassment for the government led to inquiries, but the bureaucrats had not heard of her and could find "no record of Mrs. McKenzie acting for RAAF or WRAAF during or after the war" (Dufty, 2020, p. 93). And neither the Civil Aviation nor the government was willing to assist with alternative accommodation for the company.

She briefly moved over to another property in 1953, but then shortly after decided to sell her properties and close shop. Maybe it was time to pursue her other interests in academic study, botany, and interestingly enough, making and preserving jams. Even so, she still helped those few students who needed extra help from her home in Greenwich.

There are some interesting stories about her correspondence with a certain Albert Einstein in the post-war years. They began writing to each other in 1949, with McKenzie wishing Einstein a fast recovery from gallbladder surgery. Reportedly over the course of a few years, they became quite acquainted (Einstein understandably seeing something brilliant about her) where she had gifted him a didgeridoo and a boomerang. She says in a later interview:

> "He was very interested in Australia and his favourite daughter, she was really his step-daughter… was terribly fond of shells. And I used to get my marine boys to bring me in shells

from the islands, and the air boys, they'd take a big tin of shells over to the States for me." She also recalled writing to Einstein about the boomerang saying, "Some of your mathematical friends might like to plot its flight!"

(Feyne, 2020, para. 56)

We do not know as much as we would like about this interesting correspondence between the two, but we do know that there was an influence on McKenzie's life and work by the great thinker.

It is valuable to remember that during all the years of training, she never took home a salary and most likely solely relied on her husband's paycheck to make ends meet. She was frugal and sacrificed many of her own needs for those of others.

Life slowed down considerably after she retired. Her husband of 34 years died in 1958, and she moved out of her house to live over at the nearby Glenwood Nursing home.

In 1964 she was given the honor of the patroness of the Ex-WRANS Association. Then in 1976, she suffered a debilitating stroke that required her to use a wheelchair for the remaining six years of her life. During this time, she was made a member of the Royal Naval Amateur Radio Society.

In 1982, she passed away peacefully in her sleep at the nursing home at the age of 92.

## Her Legacy

Violet McKenzie cared deeply for the cause of women, and maybe unlike the women in the previous chapters who performed their tasks well and showed their resolve through their work, McKenzie demonstrated something different. She didn't just passively influence other women, she literally pushed them in the right direction. Her actions were critical to the liberties many women share today.

McKenzie was not just a pioneer, but also an advocate for the inclusion of female minds and hands in practical world matters, entirely dismissing the notions that women were to be only "clerical assistants and other kinds of handmaidens to males" (Rees, 2020, para. 51).

And for them to be able to succeed, she needed to give her service selflessly. This can be surmised by looking at an interview given years earlier, where Violet McKenzie was asked why she did what she did. "The boys deserve it," was her humbling response to which the journalist replies, "But what does Mrs. Mac deserve?" (Dufty, 2020, p. 23). A fair question indeed.

"By elevating women, we elevate society" (Dufty, 2020, p. 175) were Violet McKenzie's own words in the early 1930s.

In one of her final memoirs, we see an entry written two days before her death saying:

> "It is finished, and I have proved to them all that women can be as good as, or better than men."
>
> (Freyne, 2018, para. 60)

Violet McKenzie's story challenges the expectation that women of that era should be submissive, quiet, and obedient to the male word. If you listened, you would hear see them speak with a significantly loud collective voice, even though that voice was often either shouted down or ignored.

# Chapter Seven

## Coral Hinds: Not Alone

All the stories we have charted so far have involved the characteristics of duty, love, and honor. This final chapter emphasizes these traits of humanity through the work of Australian code-breaking women.

Coral Hinds is at the forefront of her work in code breaking, but she is not alone. We must also address Judith Carson, the first female cryptanalyst in Australia, Joan Sanders Majithia, a brilliant Australian-Indian codebreaker, and Kathleen Quan Mane, a talented Chinese-Australian decoder of Japanese messages.

Most of the stories we have touched on have highlighted the achievements of Caucasian women, but the role of women who were half nationals or minorities must not be forgotten. Added to gender invisibility were their struggles within the social system, and they faced a double layer of prejudice.

## Their Early Lives

As we have seen from the previous chapter, the early lives of these women were greatly defined by the Great Depression. Australia was just now getting a handle on its own economy and was not really prepared for the arrival of WWII.

It is important to remember that Australia in the early 20th Century was very different from her Empire. The customs, accents, and lifestyles were altering into what is recognized today as uniquely Aussie.

Australians were molded by their rugged country, and their concerns surrounded the struggle for independence from Great Britain and their new reliance on their own economy. This young country was still expected to fight for the British Empire if it went to war. A question of loyalty between Australia and Great Britain was underway, with citizens still unsure of where their patriotism lay.

Australian women in WWI contributed through charitable and patriotic funding, always relatively far from the front line and far more involved in the home front. If it was not fundraising and nursing, it was parcel packaging and sewing or knitting: "The focus for much of this female wartime civilian activity was not just the Australian serviceman, but also his dependents, and the wounded and maimed" (Australian women and war, 2022, para. 3).

More than 330,000 Australians served in WWI, where 60,000 died and 165,000 were wounded. A large sacrifice. The Australian and New Zealand Army Corps (ANZAC) were instrumental in winning battles and campaigns.

## *Coral*

Coral Nancy Hinds was born in 1924 in the small town of Orange in New South Wales, Australia. Little is known about her younger years, but we do know she had a younger sister named Ruth and that her family was relatively middle class, and suffered like many others during the Great Depression in the 1930s. Interviews suggest that she had younger brothers as well, but not much more is known.

Due to the very few interviews Coral was able to give before her death, as well as leaving little to account for in memoirs, we can assess her life only on what she chose to say.

Unlike our previous heroines, Hinds was apparently not very studious nor eager to complete school. She did attend South Orange school and then a more rural school a little later before she dropped out at the age of 14.

She chose to leave school and get a job to help her family survive through the tough times. She remembers how her father used to cycle around town asking shop owners and office managers if they were willing to take on his young daughter. During this era, people lived a hard-working, no-nonsense way of life.

Hinds worked at a bakery shop and then at a grocery store as a cashier until she and her sister made a crucial decision to join the war effort and do their bit.

This tells us that we can also assess the ability of a person's code-breaking skills not entirely on a basis of mathematical or scientific interest during the war. If a person had a skill in patterns and problem solving, then they were likely to still be considered for cipher interception and transcription.

These vital skills would prove advantageous in her role in WWII.

## *Judy*

Judith Roe Carson was born in 1922 in Brisbane. She was the third oldest of four children, as well as being the only girl. Her father was educated, a practicing doctor who was one of the first graduates of Rhodes University where he studied in Great Britain. When he returned to Australia before the war, he married Carson's mother.

Carson recalls her younger years saying that she loved being the older sister who would watch out for her twin brothers and keep them entertained on their plot of land in Toowong, Brisbane.

From the age of nine, Carson attended St. Aiden's church school for girls where she graduated in 1939. She had an aptitude for mathematics and languages and was soon offered a scholarship to attend Queensland University (QU) to study mathematics, even though her greatest interests were reading Latin, French, and German.

In an interview, Carson answers the question about whether the girls spoke German at university in their spare time:

> "No, and this is the case with all the languages that I studied. I could read them all right and write them, but I never learned to speak another language. Which is actually a very important mistake. There just weren't people in Australia who could speak, in those days, foreign languages, so you just learned to read it, that's all."
>
> (Judith Carson interview, 2004)

Indeed, that is a very interesting perspective of their work in WWII, as their true use was simply to be able to quickly translate on paper and transfer the messages through without really needing to know how to converse.

Carson recalls in an interview made with the *Australians At War Film Archive* in 2004 that she had chosen to study Mathematics along with various languages because, "they had a strange system of awarding scholarships to the university heavily weighted towards science and languages," adding, "The idea was that I should have a go at getting a scholarship, and I needed to have something that had a lot of points" (Judith Carson interview, 2004). There she became a very small part of a male-dominated degree, being only one of two females in a class of 40 men.

This showed us that Carson had quite a bright future ahead of her, not necessarily in terms of finding a decent job or progressing her career, but in terms of her being purely educated and academic. She says:

> "Well, I was not meant to go to university, really, but I ended up getting a scholarship, so that's why I went. I was expected to stay at home and just have a good time, actually."
> (Judith Carson interview, 2004).

A 'good time' can be interpreted in many ways, although this points straight towards becoming a young housewife and possibly a mother.

When she graduated in 1943 at the age of 21, she was still unsure where she should go and needed some direction. She approached her mathematics professor at QU inquiring about opportunities and how she could help in the war efforts. Her professor advised her to speak to a mathematics professor in Sydney.

There she met Professor Thomas Room, a senior cryptanalyst working for the Central Bureau in Brisbane. After the successful interview, tests, and typical background check cleared, he offered, "Come along and you can do something," with the 'get on with it' attitude and confident demeanor. *Yes! There is definitely something I can do here*, Carson thought to herself.

Off Carson was sent to be trained under Colonel Sanford, who was in command of the bureau's army unit called the Australian Women's Army Service (AWAS). Here she was given the basics at her rookie camp in military training (uniform and all) before she was introduced to the world of cryptography.

## *Joan*

Joan Sanders Majithia was born in India in 1921 into a British Army family. They migrated to Australia when she was just 18 months to live on a sheep farm in Victoria.

Majithia was always good with numbers and worked in Victoria after school at a chartered accountant firm as a clerical assistant. Bored and wondering where her work could be more useful to the war, she chose to join the Women's Royal Australian Naval Service (WRANS) in 1944 at 22 years of age. She was not too sure what to expect.

We know from the previous chapter that it all started with 14 women from the WESC signaling school stationed at the HMAS Harman. But that grew considerably as the war progressed, with women infiltrating more command centers. Eventually, around 2,000 women became WRANS by working as translators, coders, drivers, and office orderlies... everything except working on the ships themselves.

*Figure 11: Two women in The Women's Royal Australian Naval Service (WRANS) uniforms*

So as Majithia was pretty nifty with numbers, she was quickly cherry-picked from the basic signaling position at WRANS to fill a space as a junior codebreaker at Fleet Radio Unit Melbourne (FRUMEL), which was also known as Monterey.

This is the beginning of her new adventure in the top-secret world of Japanese military deciphering.

## *Kathleen*

Kathleen Quan Mane was born in 1927 in Sydney. Her father Frank migrated from China to Queensland as a young boy and later married her mother, an Australian-born Chinese woman named Amelia.

Due to the White Australia Policy of the time, anyone who was not of a European bloodline or not born in Australia was technically not allowed to receive citizenship. Therefore, when Kathleen's mother married the young Chinese man, her Australian citizenship was taken away from her, and she was thus classed as a foreigner like her husband.

Quan Mane described her early life as never lacking anything, always proud of their Chinese heritage, and living a Chinese lifestyle in Australia with her other four siblings. She says, "Although we played with the kids next door, they were Aussies, real ocker, we [learned] the Australian way of life from them, but it was very limited" (Yang, 2018, para. 15).

The irony of how many of Australia's 'non-citizens' were enlisted into the armed forces is quite strong. They were not good enough to be considered Australians, but they were good enough to die for the country. Over 600 Chinese-Australian women and men enlisted in WWII.

Nevertheless, in 1945, Quan Mane, now 18, had been working as a secretary and wanted to do something different. She had always looked up to her older sister Doreen, who had already been working as a clerk general for three years, and who had inspired her to enlist in the Women's Auxiliary Australian Air Force (WAAAF).

One day she was approached by her sister: "Well, why don't you try password decipher training at WAAAF and see if you like it there. It could be a good place for you as you enjoy solving problems."

*What an idea!* she thought. She gave it a shot and got in. She explains, "Going into the service I was a bit apprehensive at first, but the girls were very nice - neither my sister nor I encountered any racism. That was a big step forward too" (Yang, 2018, para. 18).

## Their Careers

The men and women of Australia helped the rest of the world in their momentous actions of bravery. Even though WWII affected the country less in terms of direct conflict due to their physical distance from the main stage (epicenter), it still suffered great losses.

From the early days of 1942 until the last days of 1943, Australia was deep in the Pacific War in Southeast Asia. The Japanese Navy and Air Force attacked around 111 different locations in the Australian mainland, coastal shipping, and domestic airspace.

Australia's force was not large enough in number to help fight the war when it broke out, with only roughly 3,000 soldiers. So huge recruitment projects went underway to staff and facilitate the efforts to support the British Empire. This included 5,000 indigenous Aboriginal soldiers who were not even recognized as citizens.

Women were enlisting in the Women's Auxiliary Australian Air Force (WAAAF) as well as the Australian Army Medical Women's Service (AAMWS) and the Women's Royal Australian Naval Service (WRANS).

> "Before the outbreak of war in 1939, it was rare for women to work outside the home other than in domestic serving roles. As the war progressed, more and more resources were directed at the war effort, and it soon became clear that women would have to take a more active role in the workforce."
>
> (Heath, 2019, para. 2)

Women acknowledged their situation and the support they could give.

The Australian Women's Army Service (AWAS) was also created in 1941 with its sole role to relieve the men destined to fight. Women between the age of 18 and 40 were eligible to enlist but were paid a third less than their male counterparts.

## *Coral*

In 1942, at the age of 18, Hinds and her younger sister volunteered for military service at AWAS. She expressed her motivation by saying:

> "We didn't have a brother old enough to sign up, and there were lots of boys here who were going overseas and getting killed, so my sister and I decided we'd join up."
>
> (Coral Pacific codebreaker, 2022, para. 9).

Hinds showed great accuracy and general proficiency in signals training at Ingleburn Army Base in NSW as a wireless operator. That is when she is transferred to the Central Bureau in Brisbane where she would monitor Japanese weather transmissions and efficiently decode and translate them to then be sent for evaluation to senior cryptanalysts.

There, in a northern suburb in Ascot on Henry Street, in Brisbane, Coral Hinds would take part in the exceptionally secretive work. The mansion itself was known as Nyrambla Manor with expansive gardens and beautiful architecture. The neighbors were completely oblivious to what was happening next door.

The Central Bureau was an American and Australian joint intelligence organization specializing in signaling. Their key role was to decipher Japanese Imperial traffic both by air and land, and convey closely with other Signals Intelligence (SIGINT) branches in Great Britain, America, and India. This organization supported Allied Southwest Pacific Area Command, meaning it patrolled and analyzed all Pacific Japanese signals.

*Figure 12: Nyrambla Manor, Ascot, Brisbane, c. 1944-45*

Holding a small number of staff at the beginning of the war, the Bureau eventually grew to a 4,300 staff of women and men, where some were deployed to regions in the Pacific and Philippines to apply their signaling. These secretive premises are widely considered to be the Bletchley Park of Australia, equally hidden from civilian knowledge by a fake fronting name.

Author Alli Sinclair's 2021 novel *The Codebreakers* is a fictionalized account of the story of the women in the Central Bureau along with the commitments and friendships that were built there. She neatly explains the core of the organization and its recruitment with, "exceptional logic and integrity attracts the attention of Central Bureau - an intelligence organization working with England's Bletchley Park codebreakers. But joining the Central Bureau means signing a lifetime contract. Breaking it is treason" (Sinclair, 2021, p. 1).

Again, we see the importance of the work that was being done as well as the ignorance of many of these women to what the work *actually* pertained to. Hinds says:

> "There were some very important messages but we didn't always know how important they were."
> (Babbington, 2021, para. 6)

*Figure 13: Women working at Central Bureau, Melbourne, Vic. 1943-05-11*

She just thought it to be really good fun, an adventure with other women who lived and worked with her for those years.

The women in the Central Bureau didn't just decode, but also encoded thousands of messages to the ships and stations around Europe and in their Naval fleet in the Pacific. They were the core information control between the other Allies and Australia.

A notorious daily routine was to carefully place incriminating information into an incinerator and remove all evidence of work done that day; each and every day, they would decipher and destroy messages sent out to Allied headquarters.

Hinds and the other women in her station worked in a tin garage just off the main building. They referred to themselves as "the garage girls." Some worked on 12 Typex rotor machines that looked very similar to the Enigma on which they typed their messages to the other Allied stations in Washington D.C., Bletchley Park, and New Delhi.

While Hinds recalls her section of the team as:

> "We didn't do the code, we deciphered it. The message all came in five-letter groups and then we delivered them on a paper ribbon... it was all very hush-hush."
> (Coral Pacific codebreaker, 2022, para. 15)

Her team would help track down a Japanese general and in turn help close the Pacific war sooner than expected thanks to their efficient and timely work.

Interestingly enough, Hinds would meet her future husband on the very first day she moved to "the garage girls" in 1944. Sandy Hinds worked as a signaller and cipher at the main campus, and they caught each other's eye immediately. He was to be stationed with his wireless unit in the

Philippines in a few weeks' time, so they really only had a couple of dates before he left.

Hinds recalls fondly her relationship with Sandy saying, "He just had the loveliest nature. I was the get-up-and-go girl and he was my calm. We just hit it off" (Babbington, 2021, para. 16). But alas, he left not too long after that and they would keep in touch through secretive coded messages like "Sandy sends love to Coral" (*The Project,* 2021) inserted into everyday communications between Brisbane and their Southeast Asian unit.

Apart from encrypted love notes, they also kept in touch in long letters that were always censored by the main office for obvious reasons. Within one of these messages from Sandy came the big question: "Will you marry me?" They had been out on a date only twice but who knew what the future held in such perilous times? So of course, she agreed!

Sandy returned to Brisbane severely ill in 1945. The conditions these Australian men were put through in the deep and dangerous jungles and marshes of the Pacific territories were bound to bring about deadly fevers, hookworm infestations, jaundice, hepatitis, and malnutrition. Severe rainstorms, stinging insects, and venomous snakes added to their suffering.

The couple married that very year, with Sandy looking very thin and tired but elated to be marrying this woman. "I had a borrowed dress - I was the third bride to wear it. I could have got married in uniform and sometimes I think it would have been nice, but I wanted to be a bride. It was a happy, happy day" (Babbington, 2021, para. 25), says Hinds.

When the war ended, so did the Central Bureau, which disbanded and either transferred the staff or released them from duty. The couple moved to a house in Melbourne, had four children, 11 grandchildren, and a whopping 12 great-grandchildren!

Sandy passed away in 2007 at the age of 85, after a long and beautiful 65 years of marriage. Two years later, Hinds was honored with the Bletchley Park commemorative badge given to the "Garage Girls" for their incredibly important help during the war. Hinds also applied and received her husband's war medal, which was very important to her saying, "He earned it. It was very special" (Babbington, 2021, para. 32).

In one of the interviews done with *Orange City Life Magazine*, Coral eloquently states how retelling her past is so important now because, "It all comes back to you. When you get older, you've got nothing else to do but remember" (Coral Pacific codebreaker, 2022, para. 26).

Hinds passed away in 2020, at the ripe old age of 96. A life lived saving countless other lives.

## *Judy*

*Figure 14: Young Judith Roe Carson*

Carson was the first female codebreaker in Australia, as she was the first recruited to the Central Bureau. It was already quite late in WWII and many of the systems and deciphering methods were well understood and employed, allowing her mentor, Room, to adequately train them on the basics of cryptanalytics.

She and her team were shown a large sequence of numbers and were given the task of picking up the same set of numbers recurring, understanding the patterns that were invisible to the untrained eye. "You're looking for patterns all the time, and when you get the same numbers appearing then you can guess something about the original material" (Judith Carson interview, 2004), says Carson with subtle ease.

Carson would start with Japanese weather broadcasts made over the radio waves and learn their Morse code keys or 'codebook.' They were only looking at the numbers, finding those patterns, and deciphering them, not needing to know the language itself.

Professor Room would then evaluate the code and determine if it was important or not. Room was said to be a very shy and reclusive type of teacher, not always easy to reason with through strict security protocols, but with a sensible and calm manner in teaching.

She learned in no time the basics of pattern recognition and started filing in more complex Japanese weather messages as the year went on. These messages were crucial for the Allied pilots to intercept while in flight over the Pacific.

The atmosphere at the Central Bureau was reportedly very jovial and young. Carson giggles as she tells, "We were all spoiled with lots of parties and dances and going to pictures and things" (Judith Carson interview. 2004), and there being so few women, they were often charmed to an excess by the overwhelming number of young officers.

Carson mentions clearly that she would not have been able to do her job if she had not been able to find the Japanese errors in their messages, like duplicates and typos. This allowed her and her team to pinpoint these mistakes in code and know for the next time what they meant. The Japanese even went as far as encoding instructions for the decipher settings to their commanders which was silly and useful, quickly being picked up by Carson. Carson then adds with a smile, "Once you're in, you're in" (Judith Carson interview, 2004).

She later received a promotion from sergeant to lieutenant within the department. She says with a smile, "It was a sort of technical appointment. I could never more have commanded a group of men than fly. It was just laughable really, they just paid me a bit more" (Judith Carson interview, 2004).

When the war was over, Carson taught mathematics at New England University College until 1947. Here she would meet her first husband, Eric, a theater performer and producer who lived in Adelaide. She recalls, "He was a very nice man, Eric. I was absolutely overcome because he was such a marvelous speaker and he knew so much about literature and politics of which I knew nothing" (Judith Carson interview, 2004). They married a year later, in 1948, and had their first child in 1950.

Carson stopped teaching after that and stayed at home for some time until her husband Eric had a chance to go on study leave to Britain, thanks to his position as a senior lecturer at Adelaide University.

The couple and their three children traveled to London in 1960, and then in 1967, each time for a year or so. Carson would later get teaching jobs at various schools there, learning their new and novel mathematics curriculum each time. She returned to Australia and got a position as a math teacher at a Presbyterian school there.

*Figure 15: Judith and Eric Wedding, 1948*

During the post-war years, she and Eric were spied on continuously by the Australian government agencies, who were worried about her revealing information. There was some outrage about the Carsons being accused of sympathizing with Communists, which irritated them, as they were both relative pacifists.

The information after her life here is a little sparse, but what we do know is that Eric died some years later at the age of 55 from a heart attack while playing a game of squash.

Then she remarried Tony Carson, a childhood friend who had been through a marriage of his own and had worked at the Central Bureau as well. They had been in contact throughout the years, him moving back to Sydney from England some years before Carson became a widow.

She said, "When you know someone when you're young and when they're young you always keep that image. So it was very powerful. Also, soon after someone dies is just the time when you're most vulnerable" (Judith Carson interview, 2004). They married soon after.

They lived together in Perth with her three children, then moved back to Sydney in 1986. During this time Carson was studying mathematics again, each year taking on a new subject and keeping her brain active. Tony died in 1994 and she moved to a small flat on her own.

"Nobody talked about anything until the first time I knew about a lot of things, fifty years after the end of the war, 1995. There were so many documentaries and stories by people" (Judith Carson interview, 2004), Carson says. This shed light on her past more than her own memories could. She was happy she got to do what she did, especially as her friends and family could eventually talk about it.

Judith Roe Carson passed away in 2017 in her flat in Sydney, at the glorious age of 95.

## *Joan*

Joan Sanders Majithia remembers her WWII life with fondness. When she was interviewed on her 100th birthday in 2021, she said:

> "It was very exciting because we all felt we were contributing something special, and of course, we swore we wouldn't tell another soul what we were doing. The work was very time-consuming and intense, we worked 8-hour shifts, sometimes on the night watch," adding quickly with a laugh, "I liked the night watch because we could get up to a little bit of mischief."
>
> (Smethurst, 2021, para. 8)

The mischief she speaks of is just some on-the-side knitting and chatting with the other ladies in the room, as they were not allowed to talk to each other during day shifts.

There were around 80 other women in her FRUMEL unit with each given a small section of the code to decode, none knowing the complete code in full. Ironically, not knowing much at all allowed them to do a lot of deciphering. Between 1942 and 1943, Monterey compiled over 3000 reports on Japanese movements and communications.

She acknowledges that people were on edge, recalling the atmosphere as somber most of the time. "We had great perspective about what was happening around us, but of course, we had fun too. I made some wonderful lifelong friends at Monterey" (Smethurst, 2021, para. 18), says Majithia with a smile.

Majithia was discharged from the WRANS in 1946 as the blazing fire of war had gone cold. She had some time off, so she chose to pay a visit to the Melbourne Club which her uncle usually frequented. There she meets her future husband, Dalip Singh Majithia, an Indian Air Force fighter pilot stationed in Melbourne with the British Commonwealth Occupation Forces who flew the legendary British Hawker Hurricane plane.

As is customary in Indian culture, the couple courted quickly, and the parents arranged everything. They were married in 1947 on Dalips' family estate in the Indian city of Gorakhpur and moved to Delhi to start their family.

As of 2022, the married couple have two children, Mira and Kiran, the latter happens to be 73 years old. Dalip is currently holding the record for India's oldest living pilot at 102 years old and his codebreaker wife is hitting 101 this year.

Unlike many of the other women and men who worked at Monterey, Majithia is able to retell her story to friends and family, as the secrecy seals were lifted in the 1980s.

In 2010, British PM David Cameron acknowledged the efforts at Monterey, officially awarding the remaining two living members with a golden pin.

Her husband's career as a pilot during WWII was applauded and commemorated, while Majithia was happy to keep her secret close.

Joan Sanders Majithia never told her husband or daughters anything about what she did during the war until much later. Her eldest Kiran said in an interview, "My mother took her vow of secrecy very seriously. Even my father knew nothing about what she did during those years. We are very proud of her and my father for the service they gave during the war" (Smethurst, 2021, para. 19).

As of April 2022, the couple is still alive and surrounded by family in India.

## *Kathleen*

She explains her role in WAAAF as a 'cipher assistant' where "you send a message from here to some other station. We just translated English to code, or code to English. You felt important because you were doing important things. And you weren't allowed to talk about it which made you more important" (Kathleen Quan Mane, 2021).

WAAAF servicewomen supported various jobs including signals, telephony, aeronautical inspection, radar operations, meteorology, engineering, and other clerical work. The one thing these women were not allowed to do was actually fly an aircraft or provide their service in any other country.

They were to become one of Australia's largest women's auxiliary services and often raised questions about equal pay, which was a thorny issue at the time. They shared sleeping quarters in large barracks of sorts with little to no privacy.

Here they also learned all the aspects that were required of military personnel, from marches, salutes, drills, and most importantly obeying orders. "Recruits from Western Australia had to come east, traveling further than they had ever been before. Arriving in Melbourne in the middle of a cold, dark, wet, winter night made some wonder what they had let themselves in for" (*Australian women and war,* 2022, para. 52).

For Quan Mane, to be one of the first Chinese-Australian women to join the WAAAF was instrumental in motivating others. But when the Japanese lifted their white flags in 1945, the work was over. She moved to China with her sister Doreen, where they devoted 34 years, working on humanitarian work under the United Nations Relief and Rehabilitation Administration (UNRRA).

Quan Mane returned to Australia in 1979 to be with her family who hadn't seen her in over three decades. Until its closure in 2016, Quan Mane was appointed honorary secretary of the WAAAF WA branch where she worked during the war.

Her niece, Kaylene Poon, commended her aunt at the ceremony, instigating how it was not common to see an Asian within the ranks of WAAAF women, but her aunt was there! "It's nice to know that they have been recognized" (Yang, 2018, para. 38), says Kaylene warmly. Kaylene is a historical researcher working in Perth on stories from Chinese-Australian veterans of the war.

As of April 2022, Kathleen Quan Mane is 95 years of age and as far as research can tell, she is still alive and well with her family in Australia.

## Their Legacies

One thing is for sure, many of these women are dignified by their past, as an honorable sacrifice that was made by many.

"I just feel very privileged that I've been in the work that I've been in. If the war hadn't been on, I wouldn't have been where I am now," says Coral Hinds in a later interview. Her friend and old colleague Joy Grace aptly finished off with, "It doesn't sound like much, but it was a lot. And I can tell you I'm proud of it. Very proud" (The Project, 2021).

Coral Hinds was one of the few who were able to be interviewed and talk openly about their involvement in WWII after the files were declassified. She and many others show the same kind of humble attitude about their work, knowing little of its true meaning then, but knowing that it was bringing the world closer to peace.

Judith Roe Carson was a long-lived learner. Even though destiny saw her take up the role of female codebreaker in WWII, her life molded back into her passion for teaching when it all ended. She eschewed any notion of heroism and downplayed her own contribution to the war effort, content to live an ordinary life.

Joan Sanders Majithia, a woman whose life was lived within the world of her father's military understanding, made her own value seen during the time. She 'did her bit' and exchanged those experiences for a life in India with her family.

And finally, Kathleen Quan Mane, who was more than just a daughter of an immigrant Cantonese father. She was a model of inclusion into roles of service that should have overlooked racial stigmatization. Yes, she arrived late to the party, but that year of working towards something greater than herself is what probably spurred her into the years of volunteering in China.

The upheaval of war created an incentive for change and progress for Australian women in all aspects of social life, which is what women of all races gained when it was done. It took many more years for the government to address racial justice, but the two world wars naturally struck a vital chord in social evolution.

It is striking how they tell their stories with neither fuss nor boastfulness. It is as if they see themselves still entrenched in the days of secrecy, so habituated at brushing off detailed questions of their work that they have maybe forgotten many aspects of it, leaving us at the very edge of our seats.

Oral history no longer holds the position of influence that it once used to; we are bound by factual evidence, with little weight put on words alone. But thanks to these women's words after 1945, through equal pay and affirmative action, men were gradually persuaded to allow women entry into the defense forces.

It is simply remarkable to look back at their lives today and see their strength and passion for a common goal. Something our world desperately needs again.

# Chapter Eight

## Conclusion

*The dogma of woman's complete historical subjection to men must be rated as one of the most fantastic myths ever created by the human mind.*

—Mary Ritter Beard

Cryptology has played an outstanding role in the molding and improvement of cultures and society as a whole. Safe and super-fast communication and business are done with privacy and security which we take for granted every day.

And now we can see, after our journey through the realm of top-secret work undertaken during the Second World War, that being taken for granted is what women had to put up with regularly. If they were to have a position in the world of working men, then they needed to know exactly where that position was and where it would stay. But when the doors were opened, there was no going back, as women would silently show how capable they could be in tough situations, thus influencing history forever.

It is always important to remember that winners write history. Might some of the innovative beginnings and heroic feats of patriotism that we hear of often be, in truth, the acts of women appropriated by men?

We have spoken thoroughly about the impact of social change through world wars made in the Allied countries. It is worth noting that the Axis forces were impeded by not trusting their most vital resource in the strategy of war: their women.

The Allied forces came to recognize, albeit begrudgingly at times, that women's potential was ready to be tapped. They were strong, hungry for inclusion and acceptance; ready to prove their worth beyond childbearing hips and dinner on the table. The deep traditionalism of the Axis powers' ideology was too entrenched to clearly see the value of women's work.

Women working for the Allied forces reveled in the secrecy and importance of their tasks. This enabled them to stand taller, prouder than before. "Loose lips sink ships" was a popular slogan at the time and that responsibility kept mouths shut to ensure the safety of soldiers and countrymen from their own early and unnecessary death.

There are so many other women who deciphered the war in the fields of communications, cryptology, languages, and technology. Women like Agnes Driscol, Maureen Baginski, Wilma Davis, Dorothy Blum, Minnie Kenny, Barbra McNamara, and Ruth Wilson play a huge part in history. But their stories are even more elusive than the women revealed here. So many interesting stories and revelations that we might never hear, but that deserve to be told.

Normal, everyday women, who had but one outstanding variation from the rest; their endeavor to break a mold. Author Kathryn Atwood describes in her 2019 book *Women heroes of World War II: 32 stories of espionage, sabotage, resistance, and rescue* how:

> "Most of these women - the famous and the obscure - had one thing in common: They did not think of themselves as heroes. They followed their consciences, saw something that needed to be done, and they did it. And all of them helped

win a war, even though many of them paid the ultimate price for their contribution. But their sacrifice was not in vain, especially if their courage continues to inspire others to fight injustice and evil wherever they find it."

(Atwood, 2019, p. 7)

It is easy to picture them saying in chorus, "We just did our bit," with that humble, unobtrusive manner and a slight shrug of the shoulders.

Were the women of WWII inspired by those of WWI? The possibility is that the young girls whose parents and grandparents had fought in the first war were able to find inspiration from their stories, their photographs, and their overall contributions to a free world. But then again, these wars were waged by men, with women sighing in frustration and fear at another world conflict less than 30 years after the first.

There is a quote by the 18th Century Danish theologian Soren Kierkegaard that goes: "Life can only be understood backward, but it must be lived forwards."

We are always trying to understand the motivations and realities of the past, yet we know that people lived it as they had to, one step at a time, figuring it out as they went according to what was expected. Progression often equals risk, and we see that risk clearly only in retrospect.

American-German writer Deborah Feldman recalls her barriers as a child, surrounded by ideals that stigmatized and alienated women from the real world in front of them. In her 2012 book *Unorthodox: The Scandalous Rejection of My Hasidic Roots* she powerfully combs through her past, the pretenses that surrounded her upbringing, and the moral context of her position in the Jewish life as a 'girl'.

> "The louder the woman, the more likely she is to be spiritually bereft, like an empty bowl which vibrates with a resonant

echo. A full container makes no sound; she is packed too densely to ring."

(Swan, 2020, para. 9)

This is a quote she used to hear when she was a young girl living in Germany. Yiddish schoolbooks would reinforce these claims that women should be silent and stay in their place. Whatever culture we have been brought up in, most women can resonate with the pain of feeling silenced by the patriarchal society.

Women did so much more than act as mere placeholders for men. But a door opens in the distance, and a man is ushering you out. You only have a moment to look back at what you've accomplished before the door shuts behind you. Never to be re-opened or mentioned again. A quick, "Thank you for your service, Maam" and that's that. Goodbye, Sayonara, Auf Wiedersehen, and Arrivederci!

Women gently pushed aside when the work was not only done, but optimized, clarified, and condensed into a far greater body of work.

Throughout history, in countries all around the world, women are still being silenced. Just like the Joan Clarkes and Violet McKenzies of the past, modern women still have to battle for respect and recognition, as well as authority within the workplace. Change is never quick, but just as Joan Clarke heard how the Enigma was impossible to break while she helped break it, so women today continue to be dismissed while they actively engage in changing the world around them.

A celebration of the efforts of the women codebreakers of World War II efforts is long overdue. The code of silence around their work has finally been broken and their courage and achievements deserve to be immortalized.

Many men vocally proclaimed the need to go to war. Many women quietly assisted in bringing it to an end. Their codebreaking work was unlauded and understated, even by themselves. No medals, praise, nor glory for them. They could not march in veterans' rallies nor reminisce about their war years. In common with their male counterparts, they were forbidden to talk about their war work, even to their spouses and children. Many took their secrets to their graves. Yet their contribution, however overlooked, was vital.

Elizabeth Friedman, Genevieve Grotjan, Joan Clarke, Mavis Batey, Violet McKenzie, Coral Hinds, Judy Carson, Joan Sanders, and Kathleen Quan Mane are names that should never be forgotten. Their stories deserve to be brought out of the shadows into the spotlight. They gave courage to younger women following in their footsteps.

The female codebreakers of WWII featured in this book, (and there are so many others), helped pave the way for women in the fields of mathematics, science, and engineering. Many women working in these job arenas today are still subject to 'eye rolling' and dismissive attitudes; just as Violet McKenzie was. The women codebreakers of WWII were proactive, diligently applying their intellect to their work. They led by their example.

Credit and thanks are due to you, the reader, for having the curiosity to want to explore what lies beneath what is immediately apparent on the surface. Delving deeper into history not only expands our knowledge but brings wisdom into our own lives. It enables us to strategically learn the lessons of the past and reminds us not to get lost in the minutiae that distract us from the bigger picture.

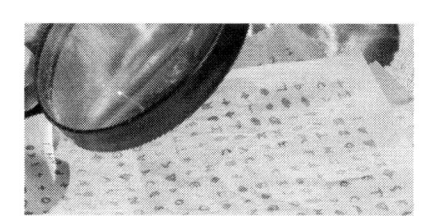

*If you have enjoyed reading this book, please take a moment to give it a quick review and rating on Amazon. This is so helpful in boosting its visibility. To make this quick and easy for you, just scan the QR code of your country's marketplace to take you straight to the 'leave a review' section. Many thanks again for choosing to read this book, and please keep your eye out for upcoming books in this series.*

*Have a look at the other books in the Brave Women Who Changed the Course in WWII and the Brave Women in History series by visiting:* www.ReadEliseBaker.com

*Sign up for Elise's monthly Brave Women in History newsletter and receive an eBook as a thank-you gift.*

US: Leave a review on amazon.com:

UK: Leave a review on amazon.co.uk

Australia: Leave a review on amazon.com.au

Canada: To leave a review on amazon.ca

## About the Author

Elise Baker has a lifelong interest in women's history and feminism. She holds an Honors degree and a Postgraduate Diploma that led to a career as a librarian, archivist, and eventually an editor for television. She loves traveling to different countries and experiencing diverse cultures. When she's not reading or writing, she enjoys walking with her dog along the beach and seeing plays at the theater with family and friends.

Elise's maternal family, from the borderlands of the Czech Republic, became refugees with no country to belong to after the Second World War and dispersed all over the world. She grew up listening to her grandmother's recollections of this time and believes that understanding and learning from the bravery of ordinary women is essential in shaping the future.

Her passion is excavating the past to unearth the stories of women whose remarkable feats and accomplishments have been buried and forgotten because of their gender. Her sincere hope is that they can fuel and inspire women of today to face adversity and discrimination with courage. Nothing gives her more joy than celebrating stories beyond the usual narratives. Their stories offer a more balanced perspective on history.

To see more books in the Brave Women in History and the Brave Women Who Changed the Course of WWII series, please visit: www.ReadEliseBaker.comor scan the QR code below.

## Also By

Other books in the **Brave Women Who Changed the Course of WWII** series:

Princess, Countess, Socialite, Spy: True Stories of High-Society Ladies Turned WWII Spies

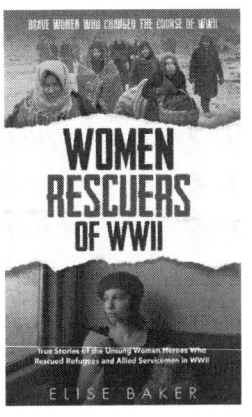

Women Rescuers of WWII: True Stories of the Unsung Women Heroes Who Rescued Refugees and Allied Servicemen in WWII

Nightingales, Bluebirds and Angels of Mercy: True Stories of the Courage and Heroism of Nurses on the Front Line in WWII

Books in the **Brave Women in History** series:

Powerful Celtic Women in History: Warrior Queens, Priestesses, and Wise Women

Voices of Freedom: Harriet Tubman, Sojourner Truth, and Other Women Abolitionists Who Shattered Chains

Blazing the Way: Match Girls, Mill Girls, and Other Fiery Females
Whose Strikes Sparked a Revolution in Women's Rights

To see all Elise Baker's books, and to keep an eye out for new titles, please visit www.ReadEliseBaker.com or scan the QR code below:

## Image References

Australia at War Film Archive. (1948). [Figure 15: Judith and Eric Wedding, 1948].

Australia at War Film Archive. [Figure 14: Young Judith Roe Carson].

Australian War Memorial. [Figure 9: Three women in WESC uniforms. Left to right: Mrs Florence Violet McKenzie, founder of WESC; Pat McInnes; Esme Kura Murrell].

Australian War Memorial. [Figure 6: Florence Violet McKenzie in WESC uniform].

Australian War Memorial. (1943, May 11). [Figure 13: Women working at Central Bureau, Melbourne, Vic. 1943-05-11].

Australian War Memorial. (c. 1944 - 1945). [Figure 12: Nyrambla Manor, Ascot, Brisbane, c. 1944-45].

Australian War Memorial. (c. 1945 - 1946). [Figure 10: Group portrait of WRANS and two sailors on staff at HMAS Harman].

Australian War Memorial. (1941, August 27). [Figure 11: Two women in The Women's Royal Australian Naval Service (WRANS) uniforms].

Australian War Memorial. [Figure 7: Three members of the Women's Emergency Signaling Corps].

Buffalo University. (1935). [Figure 3: 1935 Buffalonian yearbook: Genevieve Grotjan, Mathematics, Pi Kappa Phi].

Curry, C. (2019, October 5). [Figure 8: Old Morse Code booklet].

Gandiya, F. (2020, December 28). [Figure 1: The Colossus Computer on display at the National Museum of Computing].

Sbicego, M. (2019, October 30). [Figure 5:Enigma encryption-machine].

Mdyson, J. (2018, July 6). [Figure 4: Bletchley Park today].

National Security Agency. [Figure 2: Elizabeth Smith Friedman]. NSA website {{PD-USGov}}, Elizebeth Friedman, marked as public domain, more details on Wikipedia Commons.

## Acknowledgments

Images from the *Australia at War Film Archive* under *UNSW Canberra* granted permission to use the precious photos that were depicted in this book.

The same goes for the *Australian War Memorial* who also gave access to their images and archives.

Image of Genevieve Grotjan Feinstein courtesy of the University Archives, *University of Buffalo,* The State University at New York.

Thank you!

# REFERENCES & BIBLIOGRAPHY

Alvarez, D. J. (2000). *Secret messages: codebreaking and American diplomacy, 1930-1945 (pp. 7–10).* University Press Of Kansas.

Atwood, K. J. (2016). *Women heroes of World War I – 16 remarkable resisters, soldiers, spies, and medics.* Chicago Review Press.

Atwood, K. J. (2019). *Women heroes of World War II: 32 stories of espionage, sabotage, resistance, and rescue (p. 7).* Chicago Review.

Australia during WWII. (2019, February 28). *Military history of Australia during World War II.* Wikipedia; Wikimedia Foundation. https://en.wikipedia.org/wiki/Military_history_of_Australia_during_World_War_II

Australian women and war. (2022). *Australian women and war.* Anzac Portal. https://anzacportal.dva.gov.au/resources/australian-women-and-war#3

Babbington, E. (2021, April 22). *Aussie Anzac Day heroine: "My life as a secret WWII codebreaker."* Now to Love. https://www.nowtolove.com.au/news/real-life/anzac-day-heroine-67474

Baigorri-Jalon, J. (2011). *Wars, languages and the role(s) of interpreters.* HAL Open Science, hal-00599599(hal-00599599), 173–204. Beyrouth, Lebanon. https://hal.archives-ouvertes.fr/hal-00599599/

Baraniuk, C. (2017, October 10). *The female code-breakers who were left out of history books.*
Bbc.com; BBC Future.
https://www.bbc.com/future/article/20171009-the-female-code-breakers-who-were-left-out-of-history-books

Behind the News. (2020). *Australia's involvement in WWII*. YouTube. https://www.youtube.com/watch?v=0mshs4HLZB0

Butler, K. (2020, December 29). *How codebreaker Elizabeth Friedman fought Nazi spies.*
Www.pbs.org; PBS.
https://www.pbs.org/wgbh/americanexperience/features/codebreaker-elizabeth-friedman-fought-nazi-spies/

Chivers, T. (2014, October 11). *Could you have been a codebreaker at Bletchley Park?* The Telegraph. http://www.telegraph.co.uk/history/world-war-two/11151478/Could-you-have-been-a-codebreaker-at-Bletchley-Park.html

Coral Pacific codebreaker. (2022). *Coral was Orange's own Pacific War codebreaker.* Orange City Life. https://www.orangecitylife.com.au/home/2021/6/9/coral-was-oranges-own-pacific-war-codebreaker

Damico, T. M. (2009). *A brief history of cryptography*. Inquiries Journal, 1(11).
http://www.inquiriesjournal.com/articles/1698/a-brief-history-of-cryptography

Dearnley, D. E. (2018, June 18). *Cracking the codes of gardens: the life of Mavis Batey*. University of London. https://london.ac.uk/news-and-opinion/leading-women/cracking-codes-gardens-life-mavis-batey

Dickey, A. (2021, March 8). *The forgotten code-breaking women of WWII*. Sandboxx.
https://www.sandboxx.us/blog/the-forgotten-code-breaking-women-of-wwii/

Dufty, D. (2018). *The Secret Code-Breakers of Central Bureau: how Australia's signals-intelligence network helped win the Pacific War*. Scribe US.

Dufty, D. (2020). *Radio girl: the story of the extraordinary Mrs. Mac, pioneering engineer and wartime legend.* Allen & Unwin.

Dunlop, T. (2015). *The Bletchley Girls: War, secrecy, love and loss: the women of Bletchley Park tell their story*. Hodder & Stoughton.

Eder, M. K. (2022). *The Girls Who Stepped Out of Line: Untold Stories of the Women Who Changed the Course of World War II*. (p. 3). Sourcebooks Inc.

Elizabeth Smith Friedman. (2019, October 31). *Elizebeth Smith Friedman*. Wikipedia; Wikimedia Foundation. https://en.wikipedia.org/wiki/Elizebeth_Smith_Friedman

Fagone, J. (2017a). *The woman who smashed codes: a true story of love, spies, and the unlikely heroine who outwitted America's enemies* (pp. 14–18). Dey St., An Imprint Of William Morrow.

Fagone, J. (2017b, December 27). *World War II's best codebreaker was a woman*. Wired; WIRED. https://www.wired.com/story/world-war-2-codebreakers-elizebeth-smith-friedman/

Findling, M. (2013). *Encyclopedia of American women at war: Genevieve Grotjan Feinstein*. ABC-CLIO. https://military-history.fandom.com/wiki/Genevieve_Grotjan_Feinstein

Freyne, C. (2018, August). *McKenzie, Violet* | The Dictionary of Sydney. Dictionaryofsydney.org. https://dictionaryofsydney.org/entry/mckenzie_violet

Genevieve Grotjan Feinstein. (2020, July 23). *Genevieve Grotjan Feinstein*. Wikipedia. https://en.wikipedia.org/wiki/Genevieve_Grotjan_Feinstein

Gregg, C. (2020, February 29). *Code Girls: The Untold Story of the American Women Code Breakers of World War II*. The National WWII Museum | New Orleans. https://www.nationalww2museum.org/war/articles/code-girls-untold-story-american-women-code-breakers-world-war-ii

Haynes, S. (2021, January 11). *The story of America's underappreciated "First Female Cryptanalyst."* Time. https://time.com/5928583/elizebeth-friedman-codebreaker/

Heath, N. (2019, March 13). *How the Second World War changed the game for Australian women*. Topics.

https://www.sbs.com.au/voices/article/how-the-second-world-war-changed-the-game-for-australian-women/bca1tjodc

Herndon, J. M. (2017). *The geese that laid the golden eggs: British Intelligence and the men and women of Bletchley Park.* www.academia.edu, HIST 4900. https://www.academia.edu/32769124/TheGeesethatLaidtheGoldenEggs_BritishIntelligenceandtheMenandWomenofBletchleyPark

Higgins, M. (2016, May 12). *8 Feminist Quotes From The 1940s That Are Still Relevant Today.* Bustle; Bustle. https://www.bustle.com/articles/159736-8-feminist-quotes-from-the-1940s-that-are-still-relevant-today

Joan Clarke. (2020, April 15). *Joan Clarke.* Wikipedia. https://en.wikipedia.org/wiki/Joan_Clarke

Judith Carson interview. (2004, May 6). *Judith Carson.* Australians at War Film Archive. https://australiansatwarfilmarchive.unsw.edu.au/archive/1870-judith-carson

Kathleen Quan Mane. (2021, April 19). *Anzac Day series – Kathleen Quan Mane (English).* Australian Values. https://www.australian-values.gov.au/anzac-day-series-kathleen-quan-mane-english/

Kenny, H. (2018, September). *Central Bureau Intelligence Corps – Association newsletter.* Central Bureau Intelligence Corps, 5–7.

Lesser Known Faces. (2021, January 19). *Joan Clarke - WW2 Enigma codebreaker.* www.youtube.com. https://www.youtube.com/watch?v=5y-0eq5GOSY

Leto, L., & Wilcox, J. (2018, March 29). *Pioneering women in cryptology.* National Air and Space Museum. https://airandspace.si.edu/stories/editorial/pioneering-women-cryptology

Liptrott, J. (2016, September 2). *Biography: Mavis Batey - Code-Breaker.* The Heroine Collective. http://www.theheroinecollective.com/mavis-batey/

Lord, L. A. (2020). *Joan Clarke - Biography.* Maths History. https://mathshistory.st-andrews.ac.uk/Biographies/Clarke_Joan/

Mavis Batey. (2022, March 14). *Mavis Batey.* Wikipedia. https://en.wikipedia.org/wiki/Mavis_Batey#cite_note-5

McGreevy, N. (2021, January 15). *How codebreaker Elizebeth Friedman broke up a Nazi spy ring.* Smithsonian Magazine. https://www.smithsonianmag.com/smart-news/new-pbs-film-tells-story-wwii-codebreaker-elizabeth-friedman-180976759/

McKay, S. (2011). *The Secret Life of Bletchley Park: The History of the Wartime Codebreaking Centre by the Men and Women Who Were There* (p. 6). Aurum Press Ltd.

McLaren, M. (2021, April 28). *The extraordinary life of Violet McKenzie – "Radio Girl."* 2GB. https://www.2gb.com/podcast/the-extraordinary-life-of-violet-mckenzie-radio-girl/

McSmith, A. (2008, August 19). *Women whose work saved a British convoy.* The Independent. https://www.independent.co.uk/news/uk/this-britain/woman-whose-work-saved-a-british-convoy-902894.html

Miller, J. (2014, November 10). *Joan Clarke, a woman who cracked Enigma ciphers with Alan Turing.* BBC News. https://www.bbc.com/news/technology-29840653

Mulroy, H. (2019, August 23). *Helen Mulroy meets the female code breakers from WW2.* www.youtube.com. https://www.youtube.com/watch?v=1mA-qqhEA04

Mundy, L. (2017, October 10). *The secret history of the female code-breakers who helped defeat the Nazis.* POLITICO Magazine. https://www.politico.com/magazine/story/2017/10/10/the-secret-history-of-the-women-code-breakers-who-helped-defeat-the-nazis-215694

Nelmes, M. (2012). *McKenzie, Florence Violet (1890–1982).* Australian Dictionary of Biography; National Centre of Biography, Australian National University. https://adb.anu.edu.au/biography/mckenzie-florence-violet-15485

NSA Genevieve Grotjan. (2022). *NSA historical figures: Genevieve Grotjan Feinstein.* www.nsa.gov. https://www.nsa.gov/History/Cryptologic-History/Historical-Figures/Historical-Figures-View/Article/1621585/genevieve-grotjan-feinstein/

Ouellette, J. (2021, January 12). *The codebreaker honors Quaker woman who helped bring down Nazi spy ring.* Ars Technica. https://arstechnica.com/gaming/2021/01/the-codebreaker-honors-quaker-woman-who-helped-bring-down-nazi-spy-ring/

Paterson, M. (2007). *Voices of the Code Breakers: Personal accounts of the secret heroes of World War II.* D&C David and Charles.

Peddinti, S. (2020, May 13). *The woman who shattered codes and gender barriers- Elizebeth Friedman.* www.youtube.com . https://www.youtube.com/watch?v=-7c2tDpzEXs

Rankin, J. L. (2015). *Why I love "The Bletchley Circle" and you should too.* Lady Science. https://www.ladyscience.com/bletchley-circle/ynf2fugzghrv6atla7plfnimf2iu08

Rees, P. (2020, April 24). *Mrs Mac and her codebreakers.* The Canberra Times. https://www.canberratimes.com.au/story/6728800/mrs-mac-and-her-codebreakers/

Roe, M. (2022). *Australia since 1900.* Encyclopedia Britannica. https://www.britannica.com/place/Australia/Australia-since-1900

SciShow. (2015, August 6). *Cryptography: the science of making and breaking codes.* YouTube. https://www.youtube.com/watch?v=-yFZGF8FHSg

Simkin, J. (2020a, January). *Alfred Dilwyn Knox.* Spartacus Educational. https://spartacus-educational.com/Alfred_Dilwyn_Knox.htm

Simkin, J. (2020b, January). *Mavis Batey.* Spartacus Educational. https://spartacus-educational.com/Mavis_Batey.htm

Sinclair, A. (2021, March 1). *The Codebreakers.* Amazon; Mira. https://www.amazon.com/Codebreakers-Alli-Sinclair-ebook/dp/B085DML539

Singh, R. J. (2021, March 5). *Gurugram: IAF veteran, 100, and 99-year-old wife inoculated.*
The Times of India; Gurgaon News - Times of India.
https://timesofindia.indiatimes.com/city/gurgaon/gurugram-iaf-veteran-100-and-99-year-old-wife-inoculated/articleshow/81343683.cms

Smethurst, S. (2021, August 2). *WWII code-breaker Joan Sanders Majithia turns 100.* www.dva.gov.au; Department of Veterans' Affairs. https://www.dva.gov.au/newsroom/vetaffairs/vetaffairs-vol-37-no2-july-2021/wwii-code-breaker-joan-sanders-majithia-turns

Slimming, J. (2021). *Codebreaker Girls: A Secret Life at Bletchley Park.* Pen and Sword Military.

Smith, M. (2013, November 20). *Mavis Batey obituary.* The Guardian. https://www.theguardian.com/world/2013/nov/20/mavis-batey

Swan, C. (2020, November 19). *Famous misogynistic quotes.* Soapboxie. https://soapboxie.com/social-issues/Quotes-about-Misogyny

Talks at Google. (2019, February 28). *Secret Code Girls of World War II | Liza Mundy |* Talks at Google. www.youtube.com . https://www.youtube.com/watch?v=D9sYm32TR8A

The Best Film Archives. (2013). *American Women in WW2 | Documentary Short | 1944.* YouTube. https://www.youtube.com/watch?v=QGp93ijzok4

The Project. (2021, October 20). *Secret World War Two codebreakers finally share their story.* www.youtube.com; The Project. https://www.youtube.com/watch?v=S9SfhvbloLE

Valentine, G. (2017, September 30). *From dinner parties to spy rings, "The Woman Who Smashed Codes" bursts with detail.* NPR. https://www.npr.org/2017/09/30/548666129/from-dinner-parties-to-spy-rings-the-woman-who-smashed-codes-bursts-with-detail

Van Extel, C., & Ryan, R. (2015, July 10). *Veterans of Central Bureau, Australia's Bletchley Park, recognised for top secret service.* ABC Radio National.
https://www.abc.net.au/radionational/programs/breakfast/central-bureau-veterans-recognised-for-top-secret-service/6609498

Wartime broadcast. (2017). *Prime Minister Robert G. Menzies: wartime broadcast*. The Australian War Memorial. https://www.awm.gov.au/articles/encyclopedia/prime_ministers/menzies

Wei-Haas, M. (2017, October 5). *How the American women codebreakers of WWII helped win the war.*
Smithsonian; Smithsonian.com.
https://www.smithsonianmag.com/history/how-women-codebreakers-wwii-helped-win-war-180965058/

Whitcher Gentzke, A. (2022). *An American hero - Genevieve Grotjan*. www.buffalo.edu.
https://www.buffalo.edu/atbuffalo/article-page-spring2018.host.html/content/shared/www/atbuffalo/articles/Spring-2018/features/an-american-hero.detail.html

Wilcox, J. (1998). *Sharing the burden: women in cryptology during World War II.*
Center for Cryptologic History National Security Agency.
https://www.nsa.gov/portals/75/documents/about/cryptologic-heritage/historical-figures-publications/publications/wwii/sharing_the_burden.pdf

Women in the early 20th century. (2019). *Women in the early to mid-20th century (1900-1960): introduction*. www.encyclopedia.com.
https://www.encyclopedia.com/social-sciences/encyclopedias-almanacs-transcripts-and-maps/women-early-mid-20th-century-1900-1960-introduction

Yang, S. (2018, April 23). *Her father was labelled an enemy of Australia, but this WWII veteran was given "a very secret job."* ABC News.
https://www.abc.net.au/news/2018-04-24/the-chinese-australian-woman-who-became-a-codebreaker-in-wwii/9683878

Printed in Great Britain
by Amazon

084e4046-3024-4951-9ea5-112d9991001aR02